THE CONSCIOUS COP

BALANCING ACTIVISM WITH LAW & ORDER

by
Brandon Collins

The Conscious Cop: Balancing Activism
With Law & Order

 Published by

Blue Café Books *for*
www.carladupont.com
Atlanta, GA

Printed in the USA.

ISBN: 978-0-578-30413-7

Credits
Editorial: Carla DuPont
Cover Design: Garrett Myers

TABLE OF CONTENTS

INTRODUCTION

One day, I woke up in the middle of the night and I could not fall back asleep. Sometimes this happens to me because I work overnight, so even when I'm off, my body has trouble adjusting to a traditional sleep pattern. This time was different. I couldn't sleep because there was something in my spirit that wouldn't let me. I can't remember the exact day this happened, but it was some time in 2016 as I continued to hear stories and see videos from various police shootings. It seemed as if every day there was a new story about an unarmed black man being killed by a police officer.

I know firsthand how dangerous policing can be at times. This job brings police in contact with the most dangerous segments of society such as criminals, drug addicts, homeless citizens, and the mentally ill. At times, these segments overlap one another as it is not uncommon for drug addicts to commit crimes to support their habits. The problem with society is that no one really wants to deal with the people in these particular groups, so they call the police to resolve issues for them. Therefore, unfortunately, when police come into contact with these types of citizens it is on poor terms because we are dealing with some type of complaint or criminal allegation.

When the police get involved, there is always a chance an officer has to use force, more particularly, deadly force. But, what happens when the police encounter people who don't fit into the above segments I mentioned? After all, a person who commits one crime should not automatically be labeled a criminal, just as a person who has one drink shouldn't be labeled an alcoholic. The problem comes into play when the police are conditioned to interacting with the dangerous segments, then turn around and apply that conditioning to people who deserve the benefit of the doubt.

By 2016, I had become really bothered by what I was seeing from other police officers across the country. I'd hate to pass judgement on a police officer being one myself; but let's call a spade a spade. Police departments had become too comfortable with using deadly force, especially against black men and women. While it's debatable if some of those deadly force events were warranted, most of them seem to raise an eyebrow, even for me as a police officer. When you have the consistent rate of these events taking place combined with the circumstances surrounding them, I naturally felt police were crossing a line that is hard to come back from.

I felt so bothered because I was having a crisis of conscious. Why was I having this crisis? Because I am a black man, and a police officer. I recognize times have changed over the years, but traditionally the black community and the police department have been in conflict with each other. And it's not without merit. Historically, police departments have participated in slave patrols, enforcing Jim Crow laws, and contributing to mass incarceration. So, of course the black community has a gripe with law enforcement. The question is, why does law enforcement have a gripe with the black community?

By the end of 2016, I was five years into my law enforcement career. I was having an internal conflict over my short- and long-term future, and if I should continue a career in law enforcement. The short-term answer was to stay; I was good at my job and didn't have an exit plan yet. I was good at my job because I treated people with dignity and respect, not because I made arrests. Arrests are a by-product of the job. They are not, and should not be, the measure of a good police officer.

The long-term answer, however, was more complicated and nuanced. A part of me was embarrassed, even ashamed to be a police officer. It seemed like every week a new story cycled on the news regarding the death of another black man at the hands of police. The circumstances surrounding the deaths of these men were controversial at best and atrocious at worst. Names such as Tamir Rice, Philando Castile, and Terence Crutcher come to mind and really struck a chord with me because neither of them resisted arrest. More details surrounding their incidents are discussed later in the book. Then there are others such as Eric Garner, Alton Sterling, and Mike Brown where people, especially cops, will argue that they never should have resisted arrest and they would still be alive today. Even if that were true, it still *feels* as if they were denied justice and due process.

I have had plenty of people resist arrest against me that did not compel me to lead with deadly force. So, naturally, I wonder what the police could have done different. I acknowledge that it's easy to Monday-morning quarterback their decision making. However, when it comes to so many in the black community losing their lives in the same manner, then I wonder who's really at fault here. I feel I have a duty to speak out on this.

When tragic police encounters happen to members of our community, most black people have the same thought: *this would not have happened if the person was white*. If you were to take a poll, most black folk would agree that it would not have happened. Contrarily, most white folk prefer to believe race has nothing to do with these incidents. Their consensus is generally the same: "Just comply and nothing will happen," or maybe, "Don't break the law to begin with." Sounds simple enough, right? If you honestly believe that rhetoric, then perhaps you should honestly assess if you are choosing to look the other way instead of beneath the surface of systemic racism in policing.

And yes, there is still racism in policing. It never went away. Even as years passed by and more black and other minority police officers joined the force, the racism never truly went away. It was only suppressed and dormant. Periodically, racism would rear its ugly head. Many black police officers, whether they knew it or not, would be indoctrinated into a system that sometimes included racist police tactics. Some did not care and would go overboard trying to prove themselves to their white counterparts. Many cops, both black and white, would refer to black citizens as "perps," which is short for perpetrator, meaning to be responsible for something bad. The way police officers throw the word "perp" around, however, it became a euphemism for the word thug, which is a euphemism for the N-word.

Some black cops did care, yet felt restricted in the actions they could take due to fear of retaliation. Like most people, cops work to provide for themselves and their families. Few cops are willing to jeopardize their livelihood.

Over recent years I have heard the phrase, "There is no such thing as a good cop." The rationale behind the phrase is that the so-called "good cops" don't do enough to turn in the bad cops or look the other way altogether, which makes the good ones bad by default. Some of you may be familiar with the phrase "A.C.A.B.", or "All Cops Are Bastards." The overall sentiment seems to be that good cops don't speak out against the bad ones. While I disagree with the notion, I do understand why people feel that way. Of course, they have a right to their opinions and beliefs. Allow me to provide some context.

There are a few reasons why you don't see good cops doing anything. Firstly, most police departments have policies that cops have to follow to report misconduct. Most of those policies require cops to go through their "chain of command," which is a military style structure. If a cop reports misconduct or any other issue to their immediate supervisor, then it may or may not go any further. Unless you have some rank, then an individual cop's power is limited. Going directly to internal affairs is an option when it comes to reporting corruption or misconduct, but you have no control over how the investigation goes. Not to mention, the word might get out that you made a complaint, and now you have to deal with the whispers, side eyes, and alienation from your colleagues. And if you're on the road dealing with a dangerous situation and call for backup, the last thing you want is for your co-workers to take their sweet time showing up, if they show up at all.

Another reason you don't see cops speak out is that we have strict policies against speaking with media unless you're a supervisor. We are not allowed to speak about internal department issues to press media or on social media. Most police departments monitor our social media and have policies regulating our social media presence. The consequences for violating these policies can be harsh. They can affect our paycheck if we're suspended, if not completely jeopardize our employment. It can also affect our ability to get promoted or transfer to favorable units within the department.

You won't find many cops willing to sacrifice their livelihood in order to make a point, albeit for a good cause. Let's just be honest, even if I did speak out on social media, I only have so many followers. Remember I am a cop, not a celebrity, so my platform will only reach so many people. I have made comments on social media about recent events regarding policing and the social injustices that occurred. Those comments do not reach a wide audience.

Given these factors, it would appear that good cops are complicit since we don't do or say anything about the bad cops. The good ones are being restricted by factors beyond our control, but we still say and do our part. Even with me writing this book, I am putting my career at risk. The status quo for law enforcement is held in place by tradition, unwritten doctrines or codes, and the police unions.

Then there is the other side of the coin, the law and order side of the debate. It does bother me when people use a broad brush to paint all police as dirty, corrupt, or incompetent. I take pride in my profession.

Despite what happens in television and movies, it is not always easy. Sometimes we do have to make quick decisions with limited information. Think about it for a second. You have major corporations that pay CEOs millions of dollars to make impactful decisions based on tons of research and analytics, but uniformed officers are expected to perform at the same high level with less resources, less information, and much less pay.

When cops make bad decisions, it could possibly end with a loss of life which tarnishes the whole profession. I've come to accept the fact that we won't be able to change the perception of police overnight, if at all, because every time you look up there's a new tragedy. Just when you think police perception is getting over the hump, there's another reminder of how decades, better yet centuries of oppression have reared its ugly head. Yet, we still need law and order to be a functional society. Mass incarceration, police brutality, and all the other ailments of today's society can and should be addressed, but law and order still have to be the centerpiece of how we move forward. The right people should suffer the correct consequences for their actions against their fellow citizens. Whether it's the police, sheriff's department, military, or some other entity, there has to be someone or something that will hold people accountable when they commit crimes against their fellow man.

As I write this book, most of America's major cities seem to be experiencing a post-pandemic surge in crime. It is especially true here in Atlanta, my hometown. Murder rates and violent crime are up drastically. Crime has become so bad that the people in Buckhead, an affluent town in the northeast part of Atlanta, want to form their own city with their own police department. Now, whether they should form their own town, and the racial connotations lying beneath the surface of this idea pose another conversation for another day. The fact of the matter remains that the surge in crime is leaving people in a state of vulnerability and anxiousness. If someone does me or my family wrong or causes us harm, then I want them to pay for it. In a system of true accountability, people will be punished for their crimes, especially the violent and egregious ones.

The elephant in the room regarding the crime surge is that people don't want to work in our profession anymore. Not only is it dangerous on the road, but nowadays it is just as dangerous off-duty. The dangerous atmosphere off-duty is more psychological than it is physically dangerous, which could be worse. By that I mean policing can bleed into your personal life because your family and friends know you're a cop. Most cops, even when off-duty, are frequently asked common questions about the law. Some examples are when people ask if they were right or wrong after police pulled them over, or why they were the ones who got the ticket in an accident. We also get plenty of "what if" questions that could have a thousand different answers given the scenario. Most cops have learned to deal with the questions, because over time we have just mentally accepted that people will ask. We also don't mind if our close family and friends ask because we want them to be safe and knowledgeable when they're out and about.

What bothers cops the most is when we are asked why this cop decided to shoot this person, or why did this cop violate the law and use excessive force, etc. It bothers us because we don't have an answer for it. The answer usually falls in the category of the cop being stupid, scared, or racist. Sometimes, two or more categories fit. I just hate suddenly being the representative for all cops when people, whether they be strangers or not, ask about a given situation they saw or read in the news. It is almost like when a white person asks a black person's thoughts about a given topic regarding our culture. Suddenly, that black person is the representative for the entire race. Notice I said almost, because being a cop won't compare to being black. One day, either by choice or force, I won't be a cop. I can't change being black.

Today's climate is especially tense for many groups of people. While some of these groups are new to the club, one particular group, black Americans, have had it rough from the beginning. Through centuries of slavery, the Jim Crow era, and even now, black society has been marginalized by the white majority society. The United States government plays a huge role in why they were able to get away with this. Every branch of government; legislative, executive, and judicial, participated in this travesty against black America. The executive branch, which includes law enforcement, undeniably played a key role in pushing an oppressive agenda, as there were literally laws on the books that made black people second class citizens and punished us for believing or behaving otherwise.

I wrote this book to convey a simple but poignant message to the reader: I will always choose my race over my profession. I was born a black man, because the Most High God intended it to be this way. For me to change anything about that is a dishonor to Him. With that being said, I will proclaim that I am unapologetically black, and my views and perspectives reflect my position in society as a black man who happens to be a cop, not a cop who happens to be black.

Just understand that this book is in no way meant to alienate non-black races; however, it is meant to highlight injustices that are usually perpetuated by people in none other than non-black races. This book is meant for every person and profession to understand the nuances of police work and how it affects the racial dynamic. When you finish this book, I want you to not only have an understanding, but also a connection with how policing and black communities intersect. Policing is a very unique profession. Being black in America is also very unique. The only people that seem to understand are the people within those two respective groups. Imagine being in both groups. Imagine being conflicted with knowing the history of how blacks are treated by police in America, but still feeling a need to leave a positive effect on the community from which you came. Some black people love and appreciate the fact I am a cop, while others not so much. Going forward, I'm not expecting everyone to agree with every single point I make, but I take solace in the fact that after reading this book you will be armed with new information, a new perspective, and better grounds for reasoning to disagree if you so choose.

THE CONSCIOUS COP

BALANCING ACTIVISM WITH LAW & ORDER

CHAPTER ONE

ORIGINS

I want to take you back to my childhood. I grew in up suburban Atlanta, just south of the city. I would classify my household as middle class for that time period, which was the late eighties going into the early nineties. We lived in decent house in a decent neighborhood. Both of my parents were also Atlanta natives. My father worked full-time and my mother would work on occasion. My parents divorced when I was eight and I continued to stay with my mom at our house. Our standard of living dropped a little after the divorce, but we were able to afford the essentials.

My childhood neighborhood was safe for the most part. It was also a majority black neighborhood. There were no major incidents outside of occasional car break-ins or burglaries. It was not drug-ridden or ripe with violence. You could generally walk the streets any time of day. Most of the kids in the neighborhood met in the cul-de-sac in front of my house to play baseball or any other sport if we had enough people play. The police did not constantly flood my neighborhood. They would casually patrol the neighborhood or respond to a call here or there, but I never got the sense of harassment from them. The only interaction I remember with police was if one of my parents got pulled over.

There were no police officers in my immediate family either. Later, as I grew up, I learned of distant relatives who worked in law enforcement. None of them were close enough to me to really have an impression on me one way or another. My attitude of police as a child was mostly indifferent. I did not love the police, but I did not hate them either. Most of what I knew about police came from either the adults that were in my life, or television and movies. My perception of them, similar to most children, was that they arrest bad guys. When I became a teenager, I gained a little more awareness and knew enough to avoid the police if I could help it.

Nowadays, in large part because of social media, the children of today may have a different perception of police compared to generations before them. Children today are privy to much more information at a moment's notice. Many high-profile incidents have occurred over the last several years which have prompted an awareness of police activity like never before. Many parents have been forced to speak to their children about these high-profile events and explain to their children how to interact with the police. In today's political climate, parents need to have two serious talks with their children before they become teens. One talk is about sex and the other should be about how to handle themselves around a police officer and what to do if they are ever stopped.

I have a few reasons for becoming a cop. My reasoning for becoming a police officer is not because I had this lifelong dream of becoming one. As I mentioned before, I never thought too much about them unless I was interacting with them. It is also not due to my family having generations of cops before me. The main reason I chose this profession is because I was on a mission from the Most High God. Perhaps I was destined to become a cop simply so I could write this book. As of now, I have been a cop for nine years. I have experienced all types of conditions and situations, some of which I will mention throughout this book.

Another reason I became a cop was because of

two in particular who I became acquainted with as I got older. Their character, demeanor, and approach to doing things were all traits I respected and gravitated towards. I saw how these brothers carried themselves as black men and envisioned myself in their shoes doing what they dis. One thing I noticed about these brothers in particular; they never allowed their badge or the authority they possessed to affect who they were or how they interacted with people. They were approachable, and more importantly, they did not treat strangers like suspects. I told myself if I ever became a cop, I would share that same philosophy. Naturally, I picked their brain and learned what they liked and didn't like about their careers. I soon realized my personality and skill set were a match for the job.

My last reason for becoming a cop is representation. My belief is that the majority of the police force should represent, or look like, the community it serves. Far too many cities across the nation have a majority white police force serving mostly black neighborhoods. The few cops who did patrol my neighborhood as a kid were white. When you encounter someone that looks like you, there is a natural sense of ease. It is easier to establish a rapport.

Community relations between the police and the citizens have long been strained. There seems to be no end in sight as long as events happen that make the news and renew feelings of animosity and doubt. I guess I have to be okay with that. Although it would help, I did not become a cop to be liked. I became one to serve a purpose. I don't take it personally when I hear comments like "Pig!" or "Fuck 12!" I'm actually slightly amused when I hear those words. Maybe I would say the same thing if I weren't a cop. The part that amuses me is because the same people who say those phrases will be quick to call police if their car is stolen, if their child goes missing, or for any other personal misfortune they may experience. Some people simply hate us until they need us.

Now, allow me to address the title of this book. Conscious, of course, means being aware, or awake to your surroundings. I graduated from an HBCU so I always had a sense of culture and history. However, what brought me into the forefront of consciousness is when I first read the autobiography of Malcolm X. I was 25 years old and it changed my life forever. It changed how I saw the world and my reaction to it. I knew from that moment forward I needed to find a way to become part of the solution to the ails of black America, not the problem.

An activist takes action to achieve political or social ends. This is the primary reason I became a cop. This was the action I took so I could achieve a social goal. The goal of establishing right from wrong, justice, and law and order while also being aware of the plight unique to the black community. It is possible I could have achieved this without becoming a cop, but I believe the end justifies the means. I needed first-hand experience on what it takes to enforce the law. To apply it where it was needed. I needed to know why the law works in favor of some groups, but to the detriment of others.

A community can only function if law and order are present. The people in that community or society can only operate if they can generally be safe from attacks and have a structured government. Throughout history, there are examples of foreign governments challenged and overthrown by political coups. Even the United States experienced its own coup at the Capitol earlier this year. Ultimately, and eventually, the nation regained control, but if it were successful, then who knows how things would have turned out? Whether you agree or disagree with the laws on the books, whether you want the police abolished, defunded, or supported, without some degree of order our society will crumble. America is too populated with people of varying opinions and morals to think everyone will live righteously and with integrity.

When I first became a cop, I was introduced to the 80/10/10 rule. This rule, or concept, is based on 80% of the country's population conducting themselves as law abiding citizens. These people generally make an effort not to get into trouble and contribute to society. They may have simple infractions such as traffic violations. This group has never been to prison. In the worst-case scenario, this group may have been to jail only once or twice for crimes such as disorderly conduct or driving under the influence. They are generally non-violent offenders.

The next 10% are the casual criminals. This group commits petty crimes like theft or misdemeanor assault. This group also has the non-violent drug offenders. It is possible that people in this group have been to prison, but typically this group avoids hard prison time through diversion programs set up by the courts. This group is still able to function within society and has the ability to adjust and bounce back after a legal setback.

The last 10% is reserved for the hardened criminals. The members of this group commit the most heinous crimes. These are your murderers, rapists, child molesters, armed robbers, and people who abuse the elderly and other vulnerable groups. This is where the police intervene. The police are the barrier between the lawful and the lawless. We hold the lawless accountable, otherwise the lawless would operate with impunity. In a perfect world, the police would heavily focus on the latter 10%. As you can see in today's society, the focus appears to be on the 80%, with black Americans marginalized beyond proportion. Now we have to decide if the end justifies the means. I am sure most would reply with a resounding no.

Moving forward, please keep an open mind as the reader. I will share insight into the world of law enforcement as I provide the thought process of cops and why some make decisions that end up on the news. I will provide insight as a black man experiencing life in a country that participates in systemic racism. Hopefully, by the end of this book you will understand the conundrum some black police officers feel as we pursue both justice and equality.

CHAPTER TWO

DEADLY FORCE

Deadly force, when used by police, has become a hot topic as of late. In simple terms, deadly force is when police use their firearm to shoot a suspect. When this happens, it should be because there was a serious threat to life or safety to either the officer or someone the officer was trying to protect. The problem here is defining a threat because it is so subjective. That subjectivity is why you see police avoid charges in cases where the general public can't comprehend. What I consider a threat may not be what you consider a threat. This basically comes down to an individual's perspective. Personally, anyone carrying a deadly weapon who makes an aggressive move towards me or someone else is a threat in my eyes.

Now, you have to define what a deadly weapon is and also what kind of moves are considered aggressive. Generally speaking, a weapon can range from anything – guns, knives, sharp objects, or even blunt objects such as poles. Another person may see objects such as bricks, baseball bats, or nunchaku (nunchucks) as deadly weapons. All these weapons I mentioned can kill a person, especially with a blow to the head. Also, most of the weapons I mentioned are not illegal to own or even carry in some instances. Here in Georgia, there is an open carry law. Anyone who can legally own a firearm, assuming a person is of age and not a convicted felon, can openly carry a firearm in most public places. Without probable cause or other reasonable suspicion, a police officer cannot stop that person against their will simply for carrying a firearm, as long as it is holstered.

Along with defining what is actually a deadly weapon, an officer should determine if the person he or she is engaged with poses a threat. Are they making aggressive moves such as waving a pistol around and pointing it at people? Is the person with the knife holding it in his hand with his arm raised or extended? Is the person with the baseball bat winding it up like he is about to swing? These are all factors to consider when deadly force must be used. I was taught in the police academy about three elements that must exist if an officer decides to use deadly force.

- The first element is ***ability***. Does the suspect have the physical capability to kill you? In most cases 'yes,' with the exception of small children or the extreme elderly, any able-bodied human possesses the ability to use a weapon to kill, especially if that weapon is a gun. All you need to do is point and shoot. It does not take a soldier with special training to pull a trigger. The threshold for ability is very low. If you are alive and breathing, then you basically fall into this category.

- The second element is ***opportunity***. Along with ability, does a person have the opportunity to kill you? Again, this element can also be perceived as having a low threshold. Just about anyone has the opportunity to kill if they have their mind set to do so. This element, in a nutshell, asks was the suspect in your presence? If the answer is 'yes,' then the opportunity existed.
- The last element is ***jeopardy***. Was the officer's life in jeopardy in that moment? Was there a threat to the officer's life or limb?

So here is where it gets tricky, if it wasn't so already. Many court cases involving police officers as defendants are decided using the above criteria. A grand jury can decide to indict a cop based on those elements or a jury trial can convict. In all officer involved shootings there is one specific question that the officer has to answer: Were you in fear for your life? If the answer is 'yes,' then the officer is usually deemed justified. This phrase has been repeated throughout many high-profile cases in recent history. By now, I'm sure you have heard the phrase in the news, television, and movies, "I was in fear for my life." Once an officer says that, he or she has satisfied the three elements needed to justify, in his or her mind at least, in using deadly force. The problem with this one phrase is that it's way too subjective. There is no black and white because it is all gray area here. Again, we are going back to what is perceived as a threat, and there is no clear-cut way to define a threat because it is based on what a cop reasonably believes at that specific time when they pulled the trigger. It may seem as if I am playing semantics with these words, but trust, it all makes a difference when a cop is accused of shooting someone without justification.

Here is where race, cultural background, and

experience come into play. Does a white cop from a majority white suburban area and a black cop from the inner city perceive similar threats under similar circumstances? Perhaps. However, it seems my white counterparts are quick to pull the trigger for perceived threats that were not actually real. How many times has a cell phone or wallet been mistaken for a gun? We have to ask ourselves why white cops are more anxious when they encounter black citizens compared to white ones.

If a white cop spends his or her childhood around mostly white people, then they become adults and join the police department, you wonder how have they been conditioned to see us? Most of the time their perception of us comes from media or propaganda. This can create a dangerous formula. The media does not always show the black community in the greatest light. At times, the media seems to go out of their way to make sure of that. Whether it is through movies, television, the news, or music, a non-black person's perception of black people can be skewed. Black men are depicted in media as physically imposing, aggressive, undisciplined, and generally engaging in criminal behavior. Black women are depicted as angry or ghetto. After years of consuming these stereotypes from media, the average person will become conditioned to those perceptions. That same person then takes those perceptions of black people and becomes a member of law enforcement patrolling black neighborhoods.

With full disclosure and transparency, I admit that I was actually involved in a deadly shooting on the job. This happened back in August of 2012. I had just graduated from the police academy in May of that year. After spending my first few weeks on desk duty because of an injury, I was moved to the field. I was paired with a veteran officer who was responsible for training me with still a week or two away from being released to patrol by myself.

One day, on a bright and early Sunday morning, our patrol began as usual. My training officer and I were parked at a gas station going over safety tactics. We had just stopped someone who was loitering for drugs. We cited him and allowed him to leave. Soon afterwards, a lady from across the street at another gas station came towards our patrol car frantically waving her hands to get our attention. The lady said someone was just inside the gas station threatening her and others with a knife. Then, she pointed in that person's direction. There was a man walking quickly away from the scene while looking over his shoulder at us. Of course, when someone makes an allegation such as that one, you can't just let it go or pretend it didn't happen.

I drove towards the man to cut him off and stop him for an investigation. I was driving and my field training officer was in the passenger seat instructing me on how to proceed. Once we got in position to cut off the alleged suspect, we both noticed he was carrying a knife. We both got out of the car with our guns drawn. The suspect was at the front of the car, less than ten feet away from me. The man was given commands to drop the knife, but he just stood there. He quickly walked towards me with the knife still out in his hand.

At that very instant, I did actually feel afraid for my life since a knife can be a deadly weapon when used offensively. I remember having a split-second to make a decision: either wait and see what he was going to do with the knife once he got close enough, or pull the trigger and guarantee my safety. I chose the latter, so did my training officer. I shot at the suspect several times until I saw him fall to the ground. I then remember my training officer yelling in the background. I could not make out what he was saying.

His instincts and training kicked in. He called for help on the radio and made sure the suspect couldn't get to his weapon after he dropped it. The training officer also gave first aid until the ambulance arrived. After I collected myself, I began mimicking my training officer's actions. The ambulance arrived and loaded the suspect into the back and rushed to the hospital. We later learned the suspect died before arrival.

Alright a few things are happening here, so let us unpack it. Unfortunately, for starters, there was no body camera footage of the event since my department did not have any during that time. The situation began with a citizen reporting an assault. She identified a man as the assailant trying to leave the scene. Now, we have reasonable suspicion, or a reason to stop the suspect. The suspect was carrying what is to be considered a deadly weapon. Therefore, I had no obligation to fist fight him or even use a taser because neither one was guaranteed to succeed, especially given the close distance he was from me.

The best way to meet deadly force is with deadly force. I had a split-second to choose. I chose to use my gun as the best layer of protection at the time. It was not something I enjoyed, but it was necessary. Why not shoot him in the leg you say? I was never trained to do that. All the training we do at the shooting range includes silhouettes of the torso and head. None are below the waist. I've simply never practiced shooting at the waist down and I did not think at a moment where my life was in danger to be a good time to experiment with that. Needless to say, when my department investigated the incident, my partner and I were deemed justified in the shooting. If I were in that same situation again, I would do the same thing.

I have also been in situations where I could have

used deadly force against a suspect, but I chose otherwise due to the circumstances. In one situation, for example, I was in pursuit of a suspect accused of an armed robbery. My co-worker gave a description of the suspect over the radio. I saw the guy run right past my patrol car. The suspect still had the gun in his hand. I got out the car and gave chase on foot. The suspect ignored verbal commands to drop the gun or stop running. In fact, he kept running towards a dark alley behind a building. The suspect easily could have turned around and took a shot at me if he wanted. If I would have shot him, it likely would have been a justified shooting. However, since I knew my other co-workers were not far behind me and would cover me with their firearms, I decided to use my taser. I shot the suspect in the back with the taser. He fell to the ground and dropped the gun in the process. Handcuffs were immediately applied and everyone either went home or to jail safe. I trusted my instincts in that moment and the outcome was the best anyone could hope for.

In another example where I avoided deadly force, I encountered a suspect accused of domestic abuse. The lady who called was terrified and told me her husband was still inside the apartment. She told us she was attacked by her husband and afraid of what he might do next. She informed me and my co-worker he was indeed armed with a gun. We checked the apartment room-by-room until we got to the last bedroom in the back. The room itself was empty and the window looked unbothered. The last place the suspect could be was in the closet.

I opened the door and the suspect was crouched down behind some clothes; I could not see him that well. I definitely could not see his hands. Not to mention the room was dark. I gave the suspect orders to come out with his hands up, but the suspect did not move. It would have been bad tactics to try to reach in the closet and pull him out. If he did have a gun and decided to use it, I would have been toast. I decided to give the suspect an ultimatum: either come out or the closet or I would tase him.

The suspect stayed put. I counted down from three and tased him when the countdown ended. The suspect rolled out the closet and a revolver spilled out his hand. The suspect was handcuffed and taken to jail. It would have been easy just to shoot into the closet, but without knowing for certain if he actually possessed a firearm would have been just that, an uncertainty. If I have to use deadly force and possibly take someone's life, then I need to be sure the suspect is indeed a threat.

There were other encounters where I could have used deadly force but didn't. I have only used deadly force once in my law enforcement career. So why do many cops, particularly the white ones, seem quick to use deadly force against black people? Why are these tragedies of black people killed by police happening so frequently? It seems like every day now, you can turn on the news to see another story of yet another black citizen killed by police.

This is not a new phenomenon. Police have killed black people for decades, but now with the advent of cell phones and body cameras, it is more likely to have been captured on video. It feels like this current wave of killings started with George Zimmerman killing Trayvon

Martin. Although that incident was not caught on video, it captured America's attention. George Zimmerman, who is not a cop by the way, was acquitted of murdering Trayvon Martin. The trial had a similar feel to the O.J. Simpson trial, as people were on either side of the debate with no opinion in between.

Since that trial, there have been dozens of black names added as martyrs and hashtags. The reason white cops are killing black people comes down to simply being fearful. It is a fear that comes more from prejudice and ignorance than solid factors at the time of the incident.

In Norm Stamper's book, *Breaking Rank,* he (a former white police chief) explains how white cops are more afraid of black men compared to other groups. This sentiment should not be applied to all white cops, although it seems enough of them give credence to it. Stamper goes on to say in the book, "*Simply put, white cops are afraid of black men. We don't talk about it, we pretend it doesn't exist, we claim 'color blindness,' we say white officers treat black men the same way they treat white men. But that's a lie. In fact, the bigger, the darker the black man the greater the fear."*

Although I was not totally surprised at this, I was surprised that he actually said it. As he mentioned, it was sort of an unspoken thing or a code. Some of that fear is grounded in ignorance, but most of that fear is likely rooted in racism. White cops are taught from day one in the academy, almost brainwashed in fact, that it is "us against them." If you have a room full of white cops training to go out and work within black neighborhoods, how are they supposed to compute this "us against them" mentality? Naturally, these cops will go out on the road and pit themselves against the community instead of working with it. Eventually, that leads to your Darren Wilsons, Joe Pantaleos, and Derek Chauvins of the world.

Just like the rest of country, I have my opinions on some of the high-profile officer involved shootings that have transpired over the last several years. The particular cases I draw upon were especially bothersome to me because they either involved a child or a situation where I, or any other black man, could easily see himself in any given day. Allow me to touch on some of them.

CHAPTER THREE

BLACK MARTYRS

TAMIR RICE

Tamir Rice tragically lost his life back on November 22, 2014. He died after being fatally shot by Ofc. Timothy Loehmann of the Cleveland Police Department. That officer, along with his partner, Frank Garmback, responded to a call of someone at a park with a gun. Tamir Rice was a 12 year old black child. The responding officers were both white. As the officers arrived on the scene, they approached Tamir Rice in their patrol car. Within two seconds of exiting the patrol car, Ofc. Loehmann shot Tamir twice and killed him.

Now from an officer's perspective, whenever you approach a scene where someone is possibly armed with a gun, you always approach with an extra sense of caution. You may never know who has the gun, what kind of gun it is, or other pertinent details that may help. All of this can and will add to an officer's anxiety.

The call taker, who works in communications, is the person you speak with whenever anyone makes an emergency call to 911. The call taker is responsible for obtaining as much information as possible from the caller so they can decide which first responder is needed, whether it be police, fire, or ambulance. The call taker then sends this information over to the dispatcher who assigns the call to the appropriate unit.

Unfortunately, sometimes the caller may provide incorrect information. Sometimes the caller may make up details, such as saying one party has a gun, because they believe we will have a quicker response time. Other times, the information the caller provides gets lost in translation before it is received by the police officer. It is not unusual for cops to respond to calls with no information at all other than the address and the nature of the call. As cops, we literally walk into the unknown. With that being said, it is ultimately the officer's responsibility to access any threats, determine if any crimes were committed, and decide who and if an arrest needs to be made.

In the case with Tamir Rice, the initial call to police indicated a male was pulling out a gun and scaring people. Based on the report I gathered from the Cuyahoga County Sheriff's Department, who ultimately conducted the investigation, the caller mentioned the gun may be fake, but he could not tell one way or another. The caller also mentioned that the person with the gun was probably a juvenile. Right here with this limited amount of information, there is just enough to be cautious and weary, but not enough to say this person is a significant threat to society. Also bear in mind that Ohio is an open carry state and you are permitted to carry a gun, even without a concealed carry permit. Just the mere fact that Tamir possessed a gun is not an obvious violation of law. It is up to the officer to make a determination if a crime has been committed. Here is where things went absolutely wrong.

For starters, the officer's approach was not tactical. They got way too close to a person who they obviously thought possessed a gun. I was taught from my training that distance is always your friend. When you have distance from the person you are engaging, then you have time to process and decide how to react if the situation escalates. Now, at some point you have to close that distance if an arrest is to be made, but there was no way Ofcs. Loehmann and Garmback knew they had absolute probable cause for an arrest. Therefore, there was no reason to respond so closely. For them to approach that close was a mistake from the outset because they compromised their own safety.

When Ofc. Loehmann exited the car from the passenger's side, that put him anywhere between four to seven feet away from Tamir. The report mentions Tamir having both his hands near the right side of his waist. Ofc. Loehmann then discharged his weapon. There are conflicting statements over whether verbal commands were given to Tamir before he was shot. If it only took two seconds for Ofc. Loehmann to exit the car and shoot Tamir, then I find it highly unlikely that he gave a verbal command. Even if he did give a verbal command, he gave Tamir no time to comply.

Part of the verbal command is giving the suspect a chance to comply. There is no mention in the report of Tamir ever having the gun out in his hand, it only says Ofc. Loehmann saw him reaching under his shirt. There is also no mention of Tamir ever pointing a gun at Ofc. Loehmann. If Tamir was holding and pointing the gun at the officer or someone, then those would be prerequisites for using deadly force. Again, just because someone is in possession of a firearm, especially in a state where carrying firearms is legal, does not justify using deadly force. Ofc. Loehmann, however, stayed true to form and used the foolproof phrase, "I feared for my life."

Why exactly did Ofc. Loehmann fear for his life? Was it because Tamir had a gun? Was that the first time in his law enforcement career he encountered someone with a gun and he completely panicked? Perhaps he did, but I also believe race was a factor. Earlier in the chapter I mentioned how black people, especially black men, are mischaracterized as being older, bigger, and stronger than what they actually are. In the case of Tamir Rice, there were four different mentions in the sheriff's report of how he appeared older than 12 years old. Three of those mentions came from officers of the Cleveland Police Department. All of those officers stated Tamir looked like he was in his late teens. One officer stated he thought Tamir was in his twenties.

I find this incredibly interesting. It is as if they all got together and agreed to say the same thing to push the narrative of this big, scary black man who was intent to cause harm to Ofc. Loehmann. According to the coroner's report, Tamir was over five feet and well over one hundred pounds, so I am sure he was big for his age. Every picture that I saw of Tamir, however, had him looking 12 years old in the face. Leave it to the police to play up this "he looked older" narrative, that way the public will be less sympathetic of Tamir. At this point the Cleveland Police Department is engaging in psychological warfare. They did not invent the playbook, they just perpetuated it.

Timothy Loehmann was never charged or indicted for killing Tamir Rice. Like many of you, I had a hard time digesting that. I was forced to wonder if I was in the scenario, but the roles were reversed, what would the outcome have been? If I, a black cop, shot a white kid under similar circumstances, would I be cleared of any wrongdoing, or would they put my black ass under the jail? I think we all know the answer to that.

Loehmann was eventually fired from the Cleveland Police Department. He was not fired because of the Tamir Rice shooting, he was fired because he lied on his job application. The scariest part of this whole ordeal is that Loehmann eventually got a job with another police department. The family of Tamir Rice was left without justice. My thoughts and prayers go out to them.

PHILANDO CASTILE

On July 6th, 2016, shortly after 9 p.m., Ofc. Jeronimo Yanez, formerly of the St. Anthony Police Department in Minnesota, pulled over Philando Castile for a brake light that was not working. This traffic stop led to Philando's untimely death. Most of us saw the frightful video that was live-streamed by Philando's girlfriend who was with him during the incident. How did this ordeal go so terribly wrong? Let's explore.

As a police officer, conducting a traffic stop is statistically one of the most dangerous things we do. I was once told there is no such thing as a "routine" traffic stop, despite hearing the phrase repeated through media. As I gained more experience in uniform patrol, I quickly realized why that was the case. You never know who is in the car or what they have on their mind. As an officer, you try to do little things to establish control and increase safety while doing a traffic stop. For example, I may have the driver roll down the windows before I walk up. I may shine the car spotlight in a specific place, assuming it's dark or nighttime, so the driver or occupants can't see my exact movements. When I finally make it up to where the driver is, I make sure everyone's hands are visible. I also ask that the driver make sure the radio volume is down so they can hear exactly what I am asking or instructing them to do. These are just a few things I do to minimize my risk, but it doesn't eliminate them.

Ultimately, I am in a reactionary position. My actions are dictated by what a person, or people, inside the car are doing. I have to continually access and discern if there is a threat to my safety. Only when the traffic stop is over and I allow the car to leave is when I can fully let my guard down. Until then, I have to establish control over the areas I can. Good officers are able to do this while also being courteous and professional to the occupants.

In the case of Jeronimo Yanez, he failed to establish control over one key area: himself. I believe he allowed his racial biasness to overcome reason and rationale. According to Yanez's interview conducted by state investigators, Yanez said the reason for the stop was the inoperable brake light. He also told investigators that he "thought" Philando matched the description of a robbery suspect from days earlier. Let's unpack that last sentence.

There are times where cops, myself included, have pulled someone over or stopped them because that person or car was similar in description to an actual lookout, or wanted suspect. Other times it's really just bullshit. It is just another catch all phrase used to justify why you stopped that person. There have been several times where I mistakenly stopped the wrong person, but as soon as I realize it's not the person I thought it was, I apologize and let them go. It becomes racial when white cops knowingly stop the wrong person. It is also racial when white cops stop someone who they think is the right person, but once they realize it's the wrong person, continue the investigation. Sometimes those "stops" lead to tickets or arrests. Now, in those officers' minds, the end justified the means. They feel as though they removed a criminal from the streets. They either don't know or care about the fact that if you illegally stop someone and it leads to an arrest, then you are as much of the problem along with the rest of the predators in the community.

Going back to Ofc. Yanez, I am not sure if he was speaking truthfully when he mentioned Philando matching the robbery suspect description. According to the transcript of Yanez's interview with investigators, Yanez had knowledge of an armed robbery at a convenient store not far from where he pulled over Philando. The robbery was allegedly committed by two black males.

In the interview, Yanez says he was parked near

this store when he sees a white vehicle (Philando's car) with two occupants inside it. Yanez says the driver matched the physical description of one of the robbery suspects. When asked about the physical description of the suspect, Yanez tells them he cannot remember the height or weight, but that his hair was shoulder length. Yanez then described Philando as having a distinct facial feature of having a wide, set nose, which supposedly resembled the robbery suspect.

Wow! I wish I was making this up, but you can check the transcript for yourself. Yanez doubled down on his belief that Philando matched the suspect description as he repeated that several times throughout the interview. I am aware of the running joke among white people that all black people look alike, but this is utterly ridiculous. All of this, mind you, for a corner store robbery that happened some time a week prior to the Yanez's traffic stop. Not a half hour ago, not earlier that day, but a week prior. By the way, Yanez can't remember the exact date of the alleged robbery. The reality is that Yanez racially profiled Philando, and then killed him with impunity.

As the actual traffic stop began, Yanez told the investigators he smelled marijuana as he approached the car. Yanez said he did not want Philando to become defensive, so he avoided saying anything about the marijuana to him. He then told investigators that Philando avoided eye contact with him and mumbled when he spoke. Yanez told the interviewer that Philando directed his voice away from him when he spoke. Here, Yanez is painting a picture, albeit subjective, of why he took the action that he did. It is subjective because none of it is based on hard facts, only Yanez's perception. The audio from Yanez's patrol car dash cam sounded clear to me. I could hear Philando's voice, as well as Yanez's. Either they both were mumbling or neither of them were.

Then for Yanez to suggest that Philando avoided eye contact was to play up the suspicion that Philando was guilty of something. He told the investigators that the smell of marijuana stayed in his mind. He also mentioned that he was not sure if Philando had a gun for protection against drug dealers. At this point Yanez, is laying it on pretty thick, but now you understand he has to push a particular narrative in order to create a sense of danger to justify his use of deadly force.

Right before Philando is shot by Yanez, Philando informs him he has a gun. Keep in mind Philando volunteered this information. Some cops, as part of their routine on traffic stops, ask if there are any weapons in the car. Yanez did not ask Philando if he had any guns. If Yanez was so worried about the smell of marijuana and Philando possibly having ties to drug dealing, then why not ask if he was carrying a gun? Philando volunteered this information of his own free will and accord. And he was punished for it. Once Yanez learned Philando was carrying a gun, his mind went into panic mode. Yanez told him to not pull out his gun. Philando acknowledged that by saying, “I'm not pulling it out.” Yanez then shoots and kills this man.

According to the transcript, Yanez mentioned Philando kept moving his hands around and he appeared to be reaching for something. Yanez also says it was dark inside the vehicle and that he could not see the “object” Philando was reaching for. I suppose Yanez left his flashlight at home that evening. Yanez already told investigators that he typically works the night shift, so a flashlight is paramount for situations such as that. It is part of any officer's repertoire. Instead of shining his flashlight inside Philando's car so he could better see what was going on, Yanez jumped to the incredible conclusion that his life was in jeopardy. Yanez told investigators, "I thought I was gonna die."

Yanez surmised since he smelled marijuana in the car, along with the fact he believed Philando matched a vague suspect description, that gave him justification to use deadly force although he could not confirm if Philando was reaching for a gun since it was dark. Yanez reverted to the tried-and-true narrative, "I feared for my life." Yanez also made the incredulous insinuation to investigators that if Philando had the guts and audacity to smoke in front of the little girl in the backseat and risk her lungs through secondhand smoke, then what does Philando care about his life? Again, if you think I'm making this up, then you need to check the transcript.

By the end of the interview, Yanez had described Philando as someone who was a possible criminal, intoxicated, dangerous, did not follow directions, and showed contempt for the lives of everyone in his vicinity. Yanez may say otherwise, but I believe Yanez's biasness influenced his actions which led to the death of Philando. Instead of seeing Philando as a regular motorist he happened to pull over, Yanez saw him as a bad, black criminal who was armed and dangerous. Philando was dead the moment Yanez stepped out his car. The gun that Philando informed Yanez about was found in his pocket by first responders after the shooting.

Yanez was eventually charged with manslaughter, but he was later acquitted. He was dismissed from the St. Anthony police department, but not without a buyout of more than $48,000. I can only hope Yanez never works as a police officer again. I can also only help but wonder, once again, if Philando was white, would the outcome have been the same.

TERENCE CRUTCHER

On September 16th 2016, Ofc. Betty Shelby of the

Tulsa Police Department in Oklahoma, encountered Terence Crutcher during a roadway incident. Unfortunately, this encounter turned deadly for Mr. Crutcher as he was shot and killed by Betty Shelby. Back on that fateful night, Terence Crutcher's vehicle was stopped in the middle of the road. Ofc. Shelby was actually on her way to another call, but she stopped when she saw Crutcher's vehicle in the road. Shelby encountered Crutcher as he was walking near his vehicle. On the widely seen police video, Crutcher is seen walking with his hands up by his head. Crutcher is not holding any type of weapon. Shelby is following Crutcher back to his vehicle. Her gun is out and pointed at Crutcher. Shelby is allegedly giving commands to Crutcher to stop. As Crutcher makes it to the front door of his vehicle, he is accused of reaching into the window. Shelby then shoots Crutcher who falls to ground and dies.

Allow me to unpack a few details. First and foremost, I want to state that being a police officer is a physical, hands-on job. Many times, we are required to touch people against their will. It is part of the job. At some point, anyone who goes to jail has to be placed in handcuffs. Therefore, it is a job requirement to be hands-on. When it comes to Shelby, she supposedly gave orders, or verbal commands, for Crutcher to stop walking. As Crutcher was walking back to his vehicle, Shelby had plenty of time to stop him. She could have stood between him and his vehicle or she could have grabbed him at any point. Shelby, however, saw a big black dude, and instantly became afraid.

Shelby's co-worker, who was flying the helicopter above the scene along with her husband, articulated that Crutcher looked like a "bad dude." What constitutes being a bad dude? Being black? That officer, from hundreds of feet above, determined Crutcher was a bad dude. So, I'm sure Shelby looked at Crutcher as a threat to her safety. Never mind the fact that Crutcher's hands were empty, he was walking away from her, and her back up was present. Instead, Shelby claims Crutcher was reaching into his vehicle for an imaginary weapon.

Tulsa Police insists Crutcher's window was down, but from the video it is hard to tell. Even if Crutcher was reaching into his vehicle, that alone is not grounds or justification to use deadly force. Let me clarify, a black cop could not use that as justification to shoot, but for a white female cop that is completely acceptable.

Shelby claimed she was in fear for her life. This phrase has become the police equivalent of alleging rape. There are many true rape victims throughout modern history whose claims have become tainted by the false accusations levied against innocent black men. When I hear a white cop say with a straight face that he or she feared for their life, I can't help to think how people react when I explain my own deadly force incident. Do people believe me? Do people think I'm just "one of them?" Any cop who has used deadly force for a truly justified reason, not just on paper, but in practicality, should take offense when cops like Shelby use it to protect themselves from persecution and prosecution.

To add insult to injury, Betty Shelby appeared on the television program "60 Minutes" and was interviewed by journalist Bill Whitaker. During the course of the interview, Shelby meticulously paints a picture of how she had no choice but to use deadly force.

She described the city of Tulsa as a war zone when she said everyday their department receives calls about shots being fired. According to the website neighborhoodscout.com, Tulsa did not even make the top 100 list of cities with violent crimes in 2016. Shelby went on to say Terence Crutcher caused his own death. She stated that it was basically his fault for being big, black, and scary to the point where he forfeited any benefit of the doubt of being a normal civilian in distress.

Shelby quoted a phrase that is all too common in the world of law enforcement: "I'd rather be tried by twelve than to be carried by six." This basically means I'd rather have my day in court than be dead. Truthfully speaking, I would have found nothing wrong with this phrase six years ago. I am human and I want to survive a deadly encounter whenever facing one in the line of duty. I have a family to go home to with kids who deserve to have their father in their lives. However, I have come to realize that for some police officers, this phrase is more than just some mantra or a slogan, it has become a creed, an ideology. Police officers across America, particularly white police, have used this phrase to ingrain in their mind that it is okay to use deadly force despite not being in imminent danger. Just as long as they "perceive" they are in danger, then that, itself, is enough.

Surprisingly enough, Betty Shelby was actually charged and arrested. As we all know, she was acquitted. While the family of Terence Crutcher was left to pick up the pieces, Betty Shelby was seemingly rewarded for her efforts. In August of 2017, Shelby joined the Roger's County Sheriff's Office. Two months later, Shelby's record was officially expunged. Perhaps that's why my two formal requests to obtain the police report of the shooting were denied. Shelby has also been invited as a guest speaker on more than one occasion since this tragedy. Yet again I ask, if Shelby were black and Crutcher were white, then would the outcome be the same? Let's see what happens when the roles are reversed.

CHAPTER FOUR

THE REVERSAL

On 7/15/2017, former Minneapolis police officer Mohamed Noor shot and killed Justine Ruszczyk (Damond). Noor is a black Somalian male, and Justine was a white Australian female. Noor and his partner, Ofc. Harrity, were responding to a call of a sexual assault allegation. The caller just so happened to be Justine who reported hearing cries for help. When the officers arrived, they were startled by Justine who knocked on their patrol car. Noor then almost instantaneously shot Justine from the passenger seat of the patrol car.

Noor was later charged for Justine's death. Unlike the cases previously mentioned, Noor was actually convicted in trial for those charges. Yes, he was indeed convicted. There was no acquittal. There was no mistrial. He was simply convicted of third-degree murder and second degree manslaughter. If you're like me, then you can't help but notice the hypocrisy behind this conviction in contrast to the non-convictions of the previous cases I've discussed.

The first point of order I would like to mention is that Noor, just as the others before him, stated that he "felt fear," the moment he pulled the trigger. This is supposed to be the catch all narrative that cops use to justify any use of deadly force, even if they don't believe it. During Noor's testimony at trial, he described being in a dark alley and hearing a loud noise. Noor, at the time of the shooting, believed he and his partner were under attack and that he shot in defense of his partner who was closer to harm's way. Noor testified that he reacted to the fearful expression on his partner's face. Noor stated he feared his partner might be shot as Justine, who was at his partner's window, raised her hand.

It was later determined that Justine did not have a gun, or any weapon for that matter. That fact does not change how Ofc. Noor felt at the time. It does not change his perception. He perceived a threat and reacted to it. Noor's partner, Ofc. Harrity, told investigators that he was spooked by a noise and a voice, and he too withdrew his gun from his holster. Although Harrity did not shoot, he felt threatened enough to prepare to defend himself against an attack.

This brings me to my second point, Ofc. Noor

reacted based upon his training. Noor testified about receiving training on countering ambush attacks. Noor's training is in comparison to former Ofc. Betty Shelby's training. Shelby's mentioning of her training ultimately played a role in her acquittal. Shelby did what she was taught to do when perceiving a threat. Now, all of a sudden, Noor is in a similar predicament, and he will not receive benefit of the doubt. The prosecution in Noor's trial accused him of acting unreasonable and with excessive force. Perhaps Noor's legal counsel should have argued from the angle that the shooting was just an accident.

As a quick point of order regarding accidental police shootings, I want to mention an incident that occurred in Punta Gorda, Florida back in 2016. An elderly civilian, Mary Knowlton, was shot and killed by Ofc. Lee Coel during a training exercise. Mrs. Knowlton was called on to role play during for scenario where she was to play the cop and Coel was to play the suspect. Things went terribly wrong when Coel, who was supposed to be firing blanks, fired real bullets at Mrs. Knowlton and struck her twice. A crowd of people, which included Mrs.

Knowlton's husband, witnessed the event. Mrs. Knowlton was rushed to a hospital where she later died. Both Mrs. Knowlton and Ofc. Coel are white. Ofc. Coel was charged with manslaughter, however, his trial was not until three years later. For three years Coel was free to carry on and live his life. The case never made it to trial as Coel accepted a plea deal for a lesser charge and was only sentenced to probation. Ofc. Coel never served a day in prison. In contrast, Ofc. Noor's plea deal was denied in a hearing that lasted only two minutes.

Since 2013, there have been over 6,800 people killed by police either intentionally or by accident. Between 2005-2019, a total of 104 police officers nationwide have been charged in regards to officer involved shootings. Of those 104 cops, only 35 were convicted. Imagine how many cops were not charged that should have been. Ofc. Noor fell into rare company when he was convicted in trial for Justine's death. Noor said all the right things when it came to being fearful, he just simply did not have the complexion for the protection. Noor was sentenced to just over 12 years in prison. A stern and clear message was sent to black cops everywhere; that the thin blue wall stops with your black ass. What happened to Ofc. Noor is just one instance, right? That could not and would not normally happen. I would like to believe that. Unfortunately, there are other examples.

POLICE HYPOCRISY

Back in November of 2015, there was an officer involved shooting in Marksville, Louisiana where a six year old child was killed and his father was wounded from gunfire. The father and son, Christopher Few and Jeremy Mardis, respectively, are white. The two officers involved in the shooting, Derrick Stafford and Norris Greenhouse, are black. The officers pursued a car Mr. Few was driving as they were investigating a warrant. Once the officers, along with the help of two other officers, stopped the car, they approached it with guns drawn. Stafford and Greenhouse fired 18 shots into the car as Mr. Few was accused of not complying with commands. Stafford himself stated he feared for Greenhouse's life because he felt Few was about to back his vehicle into him since Greenhouse was positioned behind it. Unbeknownst to Stafford, Jeremy Mardis was in the passenger seat. Jeremy was dead at the scene.

Unlike most of their white counterparts, Stafford and Greenhouse, were arrested and charged with murder only three days after the incident. Normally, the police chief reserves judgement of the incident until everything is known, and even then they will not publicly admonish his own officers. However, in the case of then Louisiana State Police superintendent Michael Edmonson, he did not bite his tongue. He told the press, “The badge has been tarnished.” While I agree that the death of an innocent child is always heartbreaking, to go ahead and say that about your fellow officers was a death sentence. Neither officer was afforded the benefit of the doubt. There was no one making statements saying, “We are waiting for all the facts before judging.” There was also no one blaming the victim, who led the police on a car chase knowing his young son was in the car. He should have complied, right? Because that is the narrative you normally hear when someone black is killed by police under questionable circumstances.

There was also never any mention of Mr. Few accused of being under the influence of alcohol and drugs. None of it mattered in the end because punishment came hard and heavy. Stafford was ultimately sentenced to *40 years* in prison, yes 40, on the charges of manslaughter and attempted manslaughter.

Amber Guyger, who killed Botham Jean in his own apartment, was convicted of *murder* and only sentenced to ten years. For what it's worth, Greenhouse was sentenced to seven years after accepting a plea deal and only served two. Stafford's prison sentence, however, was more than enough for the both of them.

I find it ironic how Stafford was convicted even though he told investigators that he was trying to protect his partner Greenhouse. After all, those are code words police are supposed to use when using deadly force. Stafford was afraid for Greenhouse who stumbled and fell behind the vehicle Mr. Few was driving. Stafford feared Greenhouse was in danger if Mr. Few backed up. It is ironic because a similar case happened here in my home state of Georgia.

NICOLAS THOMAS

In March of 2015 Nicholas Thomas, a 23-year-old black man, was shot and killed by Sgt. Kenneth Owens of Smyrna Police. Owens was white. Police were attempting to serve Thomas with a warrant at his job when things took a turn for the worse. Thomas, who was employed at Goodyear, was preparing to drive a car into the service bay when police arrived to serve the warrant. Thomas allegedly began to drive erratically around the parking lot. Sgt. Owens felt as though he needed to shoot at the car as it was quickly approaching other officers at the scene in order to protect them. Perhaps he thought the car would magically stop if the driver could not control the car. Needless to say, Thomas was shot and killed.

Smyrna Police Sgt. Ed Carson told the media during interviews that the officers, "Were in fear for their lives," as to why rounds were shot into a moving vehicle. There also seemed to be conflicting reports from witnesses who said no officers were in danger of being hit by the car. No other officer used their weapon other than Owens. I must ask, what threat did he see that no one else saw? At least in the situation with Stafford and Greenhouse they both came to the same conclusion to use deadly force.

The Smyrna, Georgia case was brought before a grand jury which decided that no charges should be brought against Owens as he was deemed "justified under the law." By the way, if a use of force case against a police officer is ever brought before a grand jury, then watch out. Rarely do grand juries ever decide to charge police officers. Owens was allowed to resume his normal duties. As a matter of fact, Owens was promoted to the rank of lieutenant less than a year after the incident. In contrast, Lt. Stafford from Marksville received a 40 year sentence. Stafford's claim was similar to Owens in that he was shooting at a car to protect the life of someone else. Unfortunately, a six-year-old was killed during Stafford's incident. Stafford, however, was not aware that the child was in the car when he decided to shoot. Perhaps it could be described as an unfortunate mistake. Just as it was a "mistake" when Breonna Taylor was killed by Louisville cops.

By now most people know the unfortunate tragedy surrounding the death of Breonna Taylor. This young lady was in her residence asleep when the police raided her home to execute a search warrant. Taylor's boyfriend, Kenneth Walker, who was present with her, believed the police were intruders breaking in. Mr. Walker grabbed his gun and shot in defense of himself and Ms. Taylor. The police returned fire and killed Taylor in the crossfire.

In the previous paragraph, I put the word mistake in quotation marks. I do not believe the police meant to kill Ms. Taylor any more than Lt. Stafford meant to kill young Jeremy Mardis. The end result, however, was the loss of innocent life and consequences should be levied.

When I first got hired on as a police recruit, I was told by an instructor in the police academy that I am responsible for every bullet that leaves my weapon. Well, it seems as if Lt. Stafford, who is black, and the Louisville cops who shot Breonna, who are white, were held to different standards. Some will argue that these incidents happened in different states under different laws.

Usually, when an officer says they were in fear for their life, it holds up in court. You have federal case law that sets a legal precedence, such as Graham v. Connor, which allows the reasonable use of force given particular facts and circumstances that surround it. With that in mind, either Lt. Stafford and the cops who killed Breonna Taylor should have all been prosecuted, or neither should be.

Moreover, the black community was left void of justice, yet again. Why is it that we are the ones always on the wrong end of justice? The answer is because there are two justice systems. Even in the world of police, or should I say, especially in the world of police. You ever hear of people refer to the blue line or blue wall? It exists, but only for certain people.

CHAPTER FIVE

THE BLUE WALL OF SILENCE

What exactly is this proverbial blue wall? It is the concept and ideology that all cops look out for one another. There is no written policy for the blue wall, it is an unspoken code among not only police, but the overall umbrella of law enforcement. This includes prosecutors and sometimes judges. It is an indoctrinated culture to make sure police protect each other from legal or work-related consequences. But who exactly dictates or controls this euphemistic blue wall? Because for former Los Angeles Police Officer Christopher Dorner, a black police officer, it seems the blue wall did not protect him. If anything, it contributed to his detriment.

Christopher Dorner was employed with the Los Angeles Police Department from 2006 until 2009 when he was officially fired. During his short tenure there, Dorner made formal complaints alleging excessive force and racism. The complaints were unfounded and Dorner was black-balled by his department. He was later fired as he was accused of lying in his complaint. Dorner's career and life never recovered after this.

In 2013, he allegedly went on a shooting spree

that resulted in the death of four and injuries to three others. Dorner took his own life after a massive shootout with police in California. In Dorner's manifesto, he claimed that racism in the LAPD was worse during his tenure than it was during the infamous Rodney King incident. Where was the blue wall to protect Dorner from being scapegoated? Dorner was also a decorated Naval officer with no criminal history prior to those tragic events in 2013. Yet, he was portrayed by his department, and the media, as some lunatic who flew off the rails. Dorner did acknowledge he suffered from depression in his manifesto. The onset of his illness began after his firing and subsequent treatment from his department.

Again I ask, where was the blue wall for Dorner? It was the same place it was for Mohamed Noor, which is nowhere. The people inside the blue wall use a clubhouse mentality to control who is invited inside it. Every department has its own version of the blue wall as each individual department has its own guidelines and barriers for entry. LAPD's wall may be different from NYPD's wall. NYPD's wall may vary from that of my own department. Let's take a further look.

Speaking of New York Police Department and their blue wall, I believe we are all familiar with the Eric Garner case. Mr. Garner died from the result of a chokehold applied by then Officer Daniel Pantaleo back in July of 2014 because Garner was accused of selling loose cigarettes.

Pantaleo was never charged or arrested for his role in Garner's death. It took five years before Pantaleo was officially relieved of his duties. However, his colleague Sgt. Kizzy Adonis, a black female officer, was publicly embarrassed by her department. Sgt. Adonis arrived to the scene during the Eric Garner confrontation.

According to a witness she tried to intervene by telling the other officers to "let up," but they ignored her and continued their struggle to arrest Mr. Garner. By January of 2016, the NYPD formally filed internal disciplinary charges against Adonis, which included stripping her of her gun and badge. She was accused of failing to supervise the tragic event involving Mr. Garner. Of all the officers who were there and participated in

Garner's death, only the one black officer was publicly reprimanded. The blue wall magically disappeared for her as well.

Then you have Ms. Cariol Horne, formerly of the Buffalo Police Department. Unlike the cops who were with Derek Chauvin when he murdered George Floyd, Ms. Horne, who is black, did what she was supposed to do and intervened when she saw a fellow cop breaking the law.

In 2006, while responding to a dispute call, a male suspect was arrested. During the arrest, the suspect allegedly resisted which led to Ofc. Kwiatkowski, who is white, placing the suspect in a chokehold. Ms. Horne had to physically intervene to get her colleague to stop. The aftermath from the event was not favorable for Ms. Horne. She was railroaded by her department during internal reviews and hearings. Not only was she fired, she was not able to receive her pension. The blue wall was nowhere to be found for Ms. Horne, who was only trying to do what was right.

Meanwhile, Ofc Kwiatkowski, who eventually

made the rank of lieutenant, continued to show a pattern of violence and misconduct. He was the subject of at least two internal affairs investigations. Additionally, in 2016 he pleaded guilty to a misdemeanor stemming from a police brutality case going back seven years ago.

Needless to say, Ms. Horne did the right thing. Instead of being commended, she was subjected to 15 years of retaliation from her former employer. The blue wall chose to stand behind Kwiatkowski rather than a cop who actually upheld the morals and standards of good policing.

HOWARD MORGAN

Mr. Howard Morgan, who is black, was a Chicago area cop with years of service until February 21, 2005. On that day Mr. Morgan was stopped by Chicago Police for allegedly driving on the wrong side of the road and having his headlights off (it was just after midnight). The cops that stopped Mr. Morgan were white. Mr. Morgan, who was still actively employed as a cop at the time, tried to identify himself as police. The situation escalated and gunfire erupted. Mr. Morgan was shot 28 times. The majority of those gunshots being in Mr. Morgan's back, which questions if and how long he was even a threat.

Luckily Mr. Morgan, unlike so many others, lived to talk about his encounter with the police, notwithstanding permanent disabilities. The police claim Mr. Morgan shot at them during a pat down because he was angry. There were four officers in total present. If that is true, I find it hard to believe Mr. Morgan was still able to draw his weapon while surrounded by four cops during a frisk. If Mr. Morgan was able to pull his weapon and fire indiscriminately, then I'm sure one or more of those cops would have been killed or severely wounded.

Mr. Morgan's lawyers assert that the police sustained wounds from friendly fire (when cops shoot other cops by mistake). The cops returned fire and continued to shoot until Mr. Morgan allegedly stopped shooting. That would mean Mr. Morgan continued to shoot even after sustaining multiple gunshot wounds himself, which flies in the face of logic. One witness stated Mr. Morgan was never holding a gun.

Mr. Morgan was charged with multiple felonies, including attempted murder, from that incident and went to trial two years later. Mr. Morgan was acquitted of the charge of firing his gun, but the presiding judge declared a mistrial when two jurors were unable to move forward due to sickness. Therefore, no verdict was rendered on the attempted murder charge.

Fast forward to 2012, a second trial took place. This time, however, it appears any evidence that would give reasonable doubt to jurors was not allowed in court. For instance, the fact that Mr. Morgan was acquitted of discharging his firearm was disallowed. Ballistic evidence was suppressed and Mr. Morgan's van, which contained bullet holes, was destroyed. One of the cops involved had a previous charge of falsifying testimony which was also not allowed to be mentioned in the second trial. The deck was stacked against Mr. Morgan, a man who served his community valiantly with his badge. He was railroaded in court and ultimately convicted to

40 years in prison. Thankfully, Mr. Morgan's prison sentence was commuted in 2015 by then governor Pat Quinn. The lesson for the day is that the blue wall will overwhelmingly support white police officers over black ones any given day.

CHAPTER SIX

POLICE & WHITE SUPREMACY

The historical context of white supremacy and police goes back to antebellum slavery. Members of society during that time period were hired to conduct "slave patrols," and capture or kill runaway slaves. Even in the twentieth century, police departments across America enforced Jim Crow laws which completely marginalized black Americans. Given the history, one would be naïve to think those historical factors do not impact today's law enforcement. Black people were also discriminated against when it came to working for the police.

Here in Atlanta, the first black cops weren't hired until 1948. When they were hired, they were given strict orders not to arrest white people. To make matters worse, instead of keeping this strict order internal, it was published in the newspaper for everyone to see. This essentially rendered the black cops powerless to enforce the law. The blue wall was nowhere to protect black cops.

The blue wall is just another example of how white privilege and white supremacy work. And yes white supremacy is definitely part of today's police. Even the Federal Bureau of Investigation (FBI) agrees. Back on

October 17, 2006, the FBI released an intelligence report documenting police agencies across the country have been subject to infiltration by white supremacy groups. Here's an excerpt from the report:

"White supremacist presence among law enforcement personnel is a concern due to the access they may possess to restricted areas vulnerable to sabotage and to elected officials or protected persons, whom they could see as potential targets for violence. In addition, white supremacist infiltration of law enforcement can result in other abuses of authority and passive tolerance of racism within communities served."

Outside of releasing the report, the FBI has not done much to combat that trend. A trend that is continuing through this present day, because right now, we have two different police forces in this country. We have one police force that does their job with integrity and professionalism, and another force, the "*ghost skins,*" that operates with their own agenda. The ghost skins are the cops in law enforcement who are aligned with the white supremacist movement.

When I read the aforementioned excerpt from the FBI, it immediately reminded me of the chaos, violence, and terror that occurred at the United States Capitol on January 6, 2021. Many crimes committed that day were perpetrated by groups with white supremacy ideology. Furthermore, according to a USA Today database, seven current or former police officers have been arrested in connection with those riots. Keep in mind that the cops accounted for are the ones that were caught. I'm sure there were more. These cops were so committed to their cause that they waged war on their own country. They killed a police officer in the process and harmed several more. That means they chose their white extremist affiliation over their profession. When you hear people say, "Blue Lives Matter," just understand that they don't really mean it. If they did, that police officer from the Capitol would not have gotten killed. People only say blue lives matter as a slight against black lives matter.

Based on the above knowledge provided by the FBI, I have every reason to believe actual police officers with actual white supremacy beliefs continue to permeate the law enforcement culture across the country. The general public, more specifically the black community, has every right to believe they are targeted by police. Whether that is actually true or only perceived, the damage is done.

I recall a conversation that I had with a white supervisor a couple of years ago. It was actually a light-hearted debate, but the topic was about police shootings. This supervisor said he did not believe police officers woke up on the morning of their incidents with the mind to shoot someone because they are black. And I will bet any amount of money he is not the only one to think that. The Bureau's intelligence would suggest otherwise. I do not know what Tim Loehmann, Yeronimo Yanez, or Betty Shelby had on their minds or in their hearts the days they pulled their triggers, but it is not beyond the scope of possibility that they wanted to see one less black person on the streets.

This brings me to Josh Hastings, former police officer with the Little Rock Police Department in Arkansas. In 2012, Hastings, who is white, shot and killed Bobby Moore who was a 15 year old black child. Hastings was charged with manslaughter, but the charges were later dropped due to mistrials. Hastings was found liable for Moore's death in civilian court. The fact that Hastings was never convicted is a problem in and of itself. The bigger problem at hand is that Hastings was employed in the first place.

In 2006, Hastings applied and was later hired by the Little Rock Police Department despite lying on his application. Hastings answered 'no' on his application as to whether he ever attended a meeting involving a racist or hate group organization. In the comment section of the application, Hastings explains that he attended a Ku Klux Klan meeting once during high school. That alone should have disqualified Hastings; especially since he lied about it. The upper brass at Little Rock Police decided to hire him anyway.

This hire went against the documented concerns raised by Lt. Johnny Gilbert, a black lieutenant, within that department. In a memo Lt. Gilbert sent to the captain, Gilbert questioned Hastings' maturity, decision making, and moral turpitude. He also highlighted how other applicants, particularly black ones, were denied employment over similar or smaller concerns. Gilbert concludes his memo with the following statement: "The background investigation has provided valuable information that makes Hastings an unfavorable candidate and a potential liability for the Little Rock Police Department." I salute Lt. Gilbert for standing on his morals and calling out what was clearly an accident waiting to happen. If only his department had listened, Bobby Moore would still be alive today.

It is really no surprise Hastings was hired against Lt. Gilbert's warning. Hastings' father is part of the upper brass within the department. Hastings also had at least two other relatives who worked there as well. It is a classic case of nepotism and white privilege at its finest. Hastings went on to rack up numerous complaints and violations in his law enforcement career before the Bobby Moore killing. Hastings was a walking red flag. He had been suspended, written up, and reprimanded dozens of times. The powers that be in Little Rock did not take the necessary steps to terminate him or at least remove him from the road, or field duty. Instead, they continued to allow his conduct to go lightly punished until it culminated in the Bobby Moore incident. It was only then it came to light that Hastings is part of a perpetual cycle of racism overlooked by his department, which is also a clear example of racism at work in your police force.

Hastings, through depositions, revealed how he has used the "n" word multiple times. Hastings also mentioned hearing his father commonly use the word. This was not just an issue within the Hastings household, it was department wide. Ofc. Arthur McDaniel, a colleague of Hastings', revealed that he used the word, too. Another colleague, Ofc. Todd Payne, used the n-word in a subject line of internal emails. This same officer was reportedly known to have white supremacist magazines in his patrol car. I only wish I was making this up, but these incidents are invariably true.

With all these facts and circumstances present, how can one argue against the fact that black people are intentional targets of white supremacist police? How can one honestly say without a doubt that they do not believe a white officer can wake up with the mindset to kill someone black? Now, those types of cops are smart enough not to go blow out the brains of a black person without at least some cause. But, give them at least the slightest provocation where deadly force will be at least debatable, then they will gladly use it and deal with the aftermath later. After all, history shows they are rarely charged, and when they are, they are likely acquitted.

In the case with Hastings, he was hired in spite of red flags. Other than racism, how can you explain his hiring? This seems to be evidence of a pervasive problem, not only in the department Hastings worked for, but for departments everywhere. In general, it is hard to recruit and hire law enforcement officers. It may be even harder to maintain staffing levels. The law enforcement sector is always understaffed for a myriad of reasons including pay, public perception, and personal safety. Due to these reasons, departments overlook potential red flags and hire people who would otherwise be rejected if there was not a shortage in personnel. None of these reasons excuses the fact officers like Hastings should not have a gun and badge to carry out a secret agenda they have for themselves or on behalf of a subversive organization.

In 2015, several members of the San Francisco Police Department became embroiled in controversy when many racist text messages among their members became public. Many of those text messages displayed a white supremacist rhetoric as they mentioned lynching black people and burning crosses. They referred to black people as "animals." One officer in particular, Sgt. Ian Fuminger, used the n-word in his texts. Fuminger seemed to have a special displeasure for black people. As referenced in Jeff Pegues' book, *Black and Blue,* Fuminger would literally text "White Power!" He also mentioned how Fuminger would watch black kids at his son's school "like hawks." In another text, he referred to a black acquaintance as a monkey. These text messages came to light because Fuminger was under federal investigation for stealing from drug dealers he encountered on the job. The dominoes then fell as it was revealed dozens of officers liked, shared, and sent explicitly racist texts to one another.

After a lengthy legal battle, the cops were eventually fired. Keep in mind, these are the cops who were caught. Their comfortability engaging in this type of behavior, hints towards a toxic culture that permeated their department. The Department of Justice agreed and opened an investigation which led to them finding gross violations within the San Francisco Police Department.

Racist texts aren't just isolated to the SFPD. In February of 2021, The Los Angeles Police Department opened an internal investigation into a Valentine's Day themed message saying "You take my breath away," with a picture of George Floyd, referencing the infamous killing of Mr. Floyd from May of 2020 where Derek Chauvin knelt on his neck for over nine minutes. This incident lit a fuse, rightfully so, for black America which prompted dozens of major protests around the country. This incendiary text message shared among LAPD officers highlights exactly why the black community has resentment among police. This just goes to show that no matter what happens, there will always be cops who do not respect or empathize with the plight black Americans face on a daily basis.

CHAPTER SEVEN

POLICE PATROL PRODUCTION

The primary function of any police department is to protect life and property. To "protect and serve" the communities we work for. Nowadays, it feels like police departments are far removed from working for, or with, their respective communities. Instead, police have been working against their communities. Some departments are better than others when it comes to gaining and keeping the public's trust, but collectively the perception of police is negative. How did it get to this point? It got to this point because the police allowed it through debatable practices and even shadier tactics.

Mostly white communities are patrolled, and mostly black communities are policed. What is the difference? When the police patrol a community, they try to keep things from happening. When a community is policed, then they try to make things happen. Patrolling is reactive, policing is proactive. Now, to be clear, policing a community is not necessarily a bad thing. All people in all communities have the right to feel safe and secure where they live. No one should have to worry about break-ins, stray bullets, or any issue that effects their quality of life. However, when you constantly deploy heavy-handed tactics in one community in contrast to other communities, that is where the problem lies. As long as police performance is measured by stats, this problem will continue to persist.

Just like any other job in any other field, police officers are subject to performance evaluations. These evaluations are done on a yearly basis and can determine if a raise is due to that officer. The evaluations are also taken into account if that officer wants to put in for promotion or a specialized task force or unit. While evaluations are important to document and monitor the progress of an officer throughout his or her career, there are faults in the evaluation system. For example, it is the job of the sergeant to conduct the evaluation of the line officer. When sergeants get promoted or are moved around, then the officer is subject to being evaluated by someone unfamiliar with them. In essence, the only way for the new supervisor to know how good or productive an officer has been is to pull his stats. They want to see how many arrests an officer has made or how many citations an officer has written for that evaluation period.

Of course, if an officer does not meet a certain threshold, they will receive lower evaluation marks. It will say "needs improvement," and that officer will be labeled as lazy. Now, lazy officers do exist; usually not on paper. It is more of an unofficial understanding among co-workers. A lazy officer can lead the shift in tickets written and receive high remarks on an evaluation, but his or her colleagues will know better.

What I am getting at is this, one of the root problems of why police departments nationwide have problems connecting with the community, especially black communities, is because the metrics of the job force everyday officers to vilify the communities they serve. It is an "us vs them" mentality. You have to go out into the streets and be "proactive," which basically means find someone to arrest and find tickets to write. Your job depends on it. The general public usually sees it as "a quota" we have to fill. While most departments will make it a point not to call it a quota, they impress upon officers to bring home stats. There is always this palpable pressure to make sure you are not only doing your job, but that you are *seen* doing your job. This can only come from bringing home stats. The more stats you produce, the better it looks on a sheet of paper. Until police departments come up with a different metric to evaluate employees, the communities with the fewest resources will always catch the brunt of it. Some industries should not be allowed to rate performance simply on numbers because there always seems to be fallout.

There are two examples of fallout I would like to draw your attention to that occurred in recent history. The first example is the Wells Fargo cross-selling scandal. The line-level Wells Fargo employees were accused of overly aggressive sales tactics to reach sales goals to earn bonuses or at the least retain their employment. Employees tried to achieve their goals by opening accounts without the customer's knowledge or consent, even going as far as forging signatures. Senior level employees and upper management did little or nothing to discourage the behavior, and even put pressure on their employees to make their goals. Red flags were either ignored or explained away.

Ultimately, the customers began to notice

suspicious activity and began filing complaints. By 2016, the scandal had gained national attention and Wells Fargo could no longer look the other way. The fallout cost Wells Fargo billions of dollars in fines paid to industry regulators, consumer advocacy groups, and lawsuits. Top executives were forced to resign, and a company with a strong brand name recognition was publicly humiliated.

The second example deals with the teaching scandal here in Atlanta, Georgia. Many schools and teachers within the Atlanta school district were accused of cheating by falsifying student test scores over a period of years. By 2008 rumors were swirling about the increasing test scores for standardized testing. By 2010, many educators, schools, and the superintendent were under investigation. The superintendent at the time, Beverly Hall, was accused of orchestrating a pervasive atmosphere of cheating to achieve desired results. Educators faced incredible pressure to meet goals set forth by Ms. Hall. Those who met the goals were financially rewarded, and those who did not were punished, sometimes by termination. Naturally, teachers were forced to comply with the unreasonable demands and sometimes that led to altering test scores. The ramifications led to dozens of educators getting indicted.

When it was all said and done, eleven educators were convicted. Ms. Hall was also indicted, but she passed away before she could stand trial. The integrity of a whole school district was compromised due to unfair and unreasonable standards placed on the first level employees that the people higher up likely could not achieve themselves. Just like in the first example, shame and embarrassment struck down on the Atlanta Public School System. Meanwhile, the education, or lack thereof, of countless students was compromised. One quote from the indictment read in part, "Achieving the desired end result was more important than the students' education."

So how do these examples translate into policing? The reason I decided to highlight these examples was to direct your attention to the possibility of any job that bases its performance standards on numbers will always be subject to these types of outcomes. Given a profession such as police, if the profession is supposed to be based on professionalism, integrity, and transparency, then why are performance metrics based on tickets and arrests? You are inviting trouble onto your doorstep. This should not be confused as an excuse why some police behave badly and violate the law. Ultimately, it is still an individual choice. However, when your job is to meet certain goals or "quotas", especially for police, innocent people will inherently suffer the consequences for someone else's actions.

If an officer has written 20 tickets for a specific month, but their goal is 30 and the month is almost over, that officer might feel the need to force the issue. Instead of pulling over a car that ran a red light, they may pull over a car for running a yellow one. Or an officer may see someone putting on their seatbelt leaving a gas station and decide to pull them over. While it technically may be an infraction, that officer would be less willing to show discretion and more likely to write a ticket. You can begin to see how this can be problematic.

An officer who started off good now begins to operate in the gray area. Officers can quickly go from the gray area to violating civil rights. Now you get into what we call "heavy-handed" policing. While any community is subject to this style of enforcement, it is usually the black community that gets it the worst.

FERGUSON POLICE DEPARTMENT

Ferguson (Missouri) Police Department is guilty of using heavy-handed police tactics on majority black communities. Ferguson, of course, is infamous for the Darren Wilson killing of Mike Brown. Really that incident was the straw that broke the camel's back. That incident was almost inevitable because of Ferguson's documented civil rights violations. The violations were so egregious that the Department of Justice opened an official investigation into Ferguson Police in September of 2014, a month after Mike Brown was killed. The investigation revealed violations of the first amendment (right to free speech), the fourth amendment (protections from illegal search and seizure), and the fourteenth amendment (right to due process and equal protection). Just below, I provided an excerpt of some of the findings from the Department of Justice:

"Ferguson's law enforcement practices are shaped by the City's focus on revenue rather than by public safety needs. This emphasis on revenue has compromised the institutional character of Ferguson's police department, contributing to a pattern of unconstitutional policing, and has also shaped its municipal court, leading to procedures that raise due process concerns and inflict unnecessary harm on members of the Ferguson community. Further, Ferguson's police and municipal court practices both reflect and exacerbate existing racial bias, including racial stereotypes. Ferguson's own data establish clear racial disparities that adversely impact African Americans. The evidence shows that discriminatory intent is part of the reason for these disparities. Over time, Ferguson's police and municipal court practices have sown deep mistrust between parts of the community and the police department, undermining law enforcement legitimacy among African Americans in particular."

This was a devastating assessment by the DOJ after conducting extensive research into Ferguson's department. How can a police department, who is sworn to protect and serve, get this far out of pocket? Revenue, that's how. Here's more from the report:

"The City budgets for sizeable increases in municipal fines and fees each year, exhorts police and court staff to deliver those revenue increases, and closely monitors whether those increases are achieved. City officials routinely urge Chief Jackson to generate more revenue through enforcement."

There you have it. If you ever wondered why police departments become hell-bent on tickets and arrests, it's because they have received marching orders from top city officials. While police departments have autonomy, they still have people to report to. Line officers report to sergeants and lieutenants. Lieutenants report to captains and commanders. Commanders report to the chief, and the chief reports to the mayor or city officials. The pressure comes from the top down like an avalanche. Ferguson is not the only department who engages in these practices; more on that later.

Ferguson, just like Wells Fargo and the educators

in Atlanta Public Schools, have engaged in predatory practices to obtain a goal that only stresses out the rank and file. Consequently, everyone feels the need to produce to get good performance reviews and be eligible for promotions, or to just keep their job. The civilians in Ferguson are the ones who were ultimately penalized. The report goes on to indicate that the constant drive to produce tickets for revenue have led to stopping people without reasonable suspicion or probable cause. What's worse is the municipal courts are in on the violations as well. Ferguson courts would issue arrest warrants for missing court appearances or for unpaid tickets and fines. Many other municipalities do what Ferguson does to increase revenue. Here's exactly how the courts and police put this revenue scheme into practice.

A person may receive a ticket for a moving violation, whether it's justified or not. This person is on a fixed income and cannot afford to pay the ticket up front and opts for an alternative such as community service. Because this person could not afford to miss work, they also miss their community service. Now their license is suspended. That means more fees and fines. Of course, said person still needs to get to work to support their family, so they drive anyway. They are pulled over again because of heavy-handed policing and then taken to jail for the suspended license. After serving time and coming before a judge, they are ordered to pay a fine. This person who never had the income to pay the initial fine, now falls even further behind. After a while the unpaid debt is turned over to a collection agency. If the collection agency does not receive payment, then they report it to the court. The court then issues another warrant for this person's arrest. And the cycle continues.

I have heard comments from civilians I interacted with during my career implying that individual cops get bonuses for writing more tickets. While that part is factually incorrect, it is not that far off base. Someone or some entity is getting paid, it's just not me. Let's pray that never becomes true. If so, that would make Ferguson look like child's play as cops would stop people for the hell of it just to write tickets.

Furthermore, the DOJ's report found cause to believe Ferguson policed with intentional racial biasness against its black residents. Black residents made up two-thirds of Ferguson's population, but they accounted for over 90% of arrests and tickets issued. Ferguson Police practices became so bad they were literally pulling people over without any probable cause just to see if they had an arrest warrant. The "Failure To Comply" charge seemed to be the go to charge for the Ferguson police officers. Even if they illegally stopped or detained someone, the fact that the person did not want to provide identification led to a Failure To Comply charge and the person was arrested. The actions taken by these officers were not only condoned but encouraged.

As noted within the DOJ's report, "*Ferguson Police supervisors are more concerned with the number of citations and arrests officers produce than whether those citations and arrests are lawful or promote public safety.*" This means Ferguson Police produced empty calorie stats. Their communities were no safer than any other police department that did not produce as many stats.

In addition to these violations, the DOJ also determined Ferguson engaged in a pattern of excessive force in violation of the fourth amendment. Nearly 90% of the use of force cases were against the black residents of Ferguson. Many of the use of force cases resulted in stops or detentions that according to the DOJ, "Have no basis in law." This means the stop or arrest was illegal to begin with. Even in cases where the stop was legitimate, use of force was exerted when it was not necessary. Because Ferguson was so thirsty for tickets and arrests, the likelihood for use of force cases were higher. This will be true for any police department on a hunt to drive up their numbers.

Another problem with Ferguson I found in the report is, of the 54 sworn officers Ferguson had at the time, only four were black. Yet Ferguson's black residents make up 67% of the community. Whenever a police force's makeup is this disproportionate to the community it serves, you will almost always have problems. I am sure Ferguson's officers, either consciously or subconsciously, treated the residents, especially the black ones, as less than human. When you have as many documented violations as they have, there is almost no question about how those officers feel about the residents in the community. The DOJ called it a pattern of violations. When something happens once, it is an anomaly. If it happens twice, it's a trend. If it happens a third time, then it is a pattern. After the third time, it is a part of who you are. Unfortunately, Ferguson is not the only police department where gross violations occur.

CHICAGO POLICE

The Chicago Police Department was also the subject of a Department of Justice investigation. The investigation was opened in December of 2015. The DOJ found that Chicago Police, like Ferguson, engaged in a pattern of excessive or unreasonable force in violation of the fourth amendment. Both departments have violated U.S.C 14141, a section of the Violent Crime Control and Law Enforcement Act of 1994. This section makes it unlawful for any government authority to engage in practices that violate the Constitution. The U.S. Attorney General has the power to bring civil action against any government entity that shows cause to be in violation.

Other than a public reprimand and recommendations for the departments to correct itself, no civil action is ever taken.

Regarding the Chicago Police Department, the DOJ found them to use force irrespective of the Constitution, and even their department's own policy. Many of these violations committed by Chicago police were due to the lack of supervision and guidance regarding use of force. This tells me that they either didn't know, didn't care, or didn't care to know when and how to use force. Many times, their police agency was found to use deadly force on foot chases where the suspect did not pose an immediate threat. This is in violation of the *Tennessee v. Garner* Supreme Court ruling where an officer can't shoot a fleeing felon unless they pose a threat to that officer or others. According to the DOJ, Chicago Police would chase people without suspecting them of a crime. This means, for example, if an officer on patrol pulled into a gas station or apartment complex and saw a random person start running, then that officer would get out and start chasing him or her. Assuming the officer catches the person, that stop is illegal, reckless and unsafe policing. Situations like that almost always lead to a use of force. That officer's co-workers, who likely arrived to the scene as back-up, now have to be a part of the initial officer's headache of a case.

The DOJ's report highlights a handful of cases where foot pursuits started on shaky probable cause and ended with deadly force. In each case, the person killed was accused of having a weapon, and each time no weapon was found on that person. In one such case, a weapon was found, but nowhere near that suspect's area of immediate control. Reports written by the officers were not aligned with the actual evidence, which leads me to believe the circumstances were exaggerated to make sure they were justified in their shooting. It must have worked, because the Independent Police Review Board (IPRB) found the officer's actions justified. The IPRB is an agency separate from Chicago Police that looks into excessive force cases. It seems that on at least the cases mentioned above, the IPRB either did not do a thorough investigation or just simply ignored the facts. The IPRB was dissolved and replaced by COPA (Civilian Office of Police Accountability) in 2017.

Chicago's Police Department, like Ferguson's, has a history of doing a poor job punishing officers for violations. Officers from both departments seemed to get away with untruthfulness, which is supposed to be a career ending penalty for a police officer. The rationale is that if an officer is documented being untruthful just once, then what's to stop it from happening again? That officer now has a credibility issue when it comes to testifying in trial. Even an average defense attorney can use that against an officer, then the whole case loses credibility, and the suspect charged in the case is likely to go free.

When bad and unjust behavior by police goes unchecked, you end up with incidents in Chicago such as Laquan McDonald, or most recently, Adam Toledo. Former law enforcement officer Matthew Horace did a wonderful job articulating the atrocities of Chicago Police in his book *The Black and The Blue.* He, not only points out how the police department participated in covering up Laquan McDonald's death with false statements, but also how the police were enabled by city officials. The mayor during that time, Rahm Emanuel, was in the midst of a re-election campaign and could ill afford a controversy like this to jeopardize it. So, he and the rest of the city council effectively buried the story. They chose politics over justice.

Now some people, mainly pro-police people, will say Chicago and Ferguson are isolated incidents. They will say I cannot judge a whole nation of police officers based on only two departments. If you have been reading carefully, then you'll see my judgement is based on documented facts, not media propaganda or popular opinion. Remember I said if something happens once, you can dismiss it, the second time makes it a trend. The third time establishes a pattern. So now let's look at Baltimore Police Department.

BALTIMORE POLICE DEPARTMENT

The Department of Justice completed their investigation of Baltimore's Police in August of 2016. Just like Chicago's and Ferguson's Police, Baltimore engaged in a habit of making unconstitutional stops. The vast majority of these stops were conducted on the black residents of Baltimore. According to the DOJ's report, between 2010-2015 over 11,000 cases made by officers in Baltimore were dismissed by prosecutors because of no probable cause to arrest. This many dismissed cases screams of a numbers game, where cops in Baltimore were either mandated or "strongly encouraged" to make a minimal number of stops and arrests.

While black Baltimore residents accounted for the majority of the stops, it was the white residents who were twice as likely to have narcotics in their possession. The DOJ's report found cause to believe black residents of Baltimore were disproportionately affected at every stage of enforcement. This means from the initial encounter with the line officer, uses of force, and investigations; black residents were the target. Even if the upper brass within Baltimore's Police did not explicitly say to target black residents, it was implied. This is an issue within many police departments; not just Baltimore's. They go after the low hanging fruit. There is no secret that a wealth gap exists in America. Black Americans overall are subject to poorer conditions compared to other ethnic groups. Because of the wealth gap, black communities lack the resources and education needed to arm and protect themselves from unconstitutional policing. The police departments that prey on this segment of the population do not suffer severe enough consequences to correct their behavior. All of this culminates into the lack of justice for black citizens who are unjustly killed at the hands of police.

The cities of Baltimore, Chicago, and Ferguson all have a significant black population. There are other cities across the country with high concentrations of black communities as well. All are subject to the same deficiencies within their police departments as the three mentioned here. Also note that those cities are not in close proximity to one another. Therefore, you can't write it off as regional discrimination. The perception is that the South is the most racist area of the country, likely stemming from Jim Crow era laws that the police were legally allowed to enforce during those times. The problem we have now is racist people who perpetuated Jim Crow laws migrated and spread their ideology nationwide.

When crime increases in an area, neighborhood, or city, of course people want something done. Those people can include politicians and community residents. Baltimore, like most major cities, wants to bring its crime rate under control, but empty calorie stats will not help deter crime. If anything, it is proven to increase it. Many departments like to implement the "broken windows" philosophy of policing, where the police department in that area focuses on the small quality of life issues. That approach may work for some departments, but for any major department, it's only subterfuge. This is what policing has become over the past couple of decades.

Police supervisors and other department heads just want to impress their bosses with numbers. They want their communities to look safer on paper, so officers are encouraged to produce tickets and arrests that may not be sustainable over a long period of time. A community can only feel as safe as its residents perceive it. Stats and numbers don't matter to the public. The residents must also feel safe from the police who patrol it. If the residents feel terrorized or picked on by the police who patrol it, can it really be a safe community?

I know from experience that policing can be dangerous. I have had my fair share of fights, foot chases, vehicle pursuits, and uses of force. However, I have noticed police departments take on an "us versus them" mentality, not realizing that the tactics they employ create an atmosphere of hostility towards ourselves that we, as police officers, look to avoid. When some police officers suit up for work, they actually believe they are going to war. While I am all for protecting myself and making sure I use good tactics and techniques to avoid unnecessary injury, I do believe "going to war" is the wrong mindset. The mindset should simply be that of service and humility. Just like the medieval knights, police officers have been bestowed a power and responsibility to serve with honor.

NYPD'S STOP & FRISK

Most major police departments engage in some type of oppressive tactics. Some departments are oblivious to it, other departments relish in it. For years, the police in the city of New York practiced the stop and frisk policy. This policy gave the police a wide latitude in stopping, questioning, and searching citizens under the pretext of "reasonable suspicion." If you don't know, there are really only two reasons a person is required to stop for the police. The first reason is probable cause, which means an officer has either witnessed a crime or has enough knowledge or evidence to suspect a person of committing a crime. Under probable cause an officer can make an immediate arrest because it is likely this person committed said crime.

The second reason is reasonable suspicion, where an officer reasonably believes a person is committing a crime, just committed one, or about to commit one. While both reasons may seem slightly similar, the difference is that an officer cannot arrest a person off reasonable suspicion alone. Reasonable suspicion only gives an officer the right to stop that person. Whether probable cause is developed during the investigation determines if an arrest is made.

The problem with the way NYPD enforced its stop and frisk policy is how they determined who was reasonably suspicious. Since reasonable suspicion is more subjective and has a lower threshold to meet than probable cause, the NYPD can operate in the gray area without consequence. After all, who better than a police officer can determine what is suspicious? At least that is the logic used if a police officer has to testify in court. That is when you hear phrases on police reports or court statements such as, "I noticed a bulge in his pocket," or "He displayed furtive movements and avoided eye contact with me."

Now, a good police officer with genuine motives will use the above statement as clues that something is wrong and to use caution as you proceed. For an officer with sketchy motives, it is just a catch-all phrase used to justify a search, an arrest, or possible deadly force if it goes that far. The NYPD is not the only organization guilty of this. The problem is nationwide. To be honest about it, many officers don't even know they are guilty of it. Believe it or not, there are officers who don't know the difference between probable cause and reasonable suspicion. I won't claim to know every law on the books; there are too many to know. These two, probable cause and reasonable suspicion, are the pillars of lawful policing. If you can't articulate the difference, then how can you lawfully police? It's like a doctor who can't tell the difference between heart rate and blood pressure.

Let's go back to stop and frisk. Of course the idea was to lower the crime rate; but, Black and Latino communities paid the price by being harassed and mistreated. Yes, crime did go down in New York while the policy was enacted, but the end does not justify the means. NYPD abused the definition of reasonable suspicion and stopped anyone they needed to. Maybe the street officers were under pressure from their superiors to make a certain number of stops per day. That's usually how it goes. Due to politics, the department overall was pressured by the mayor's office to bring down crime.

New York is equally diverse. Like other cities, New York has areas where there may be a high concentration of one demographic. It should go without saying that the police department knows the demographics of a particular area. This information is factored in when police officials have their crime meetings and implement their strategies. It is no mistake when the NYPD targets the areas highly concentrated by the black population. Black residents seemed to be the disproportionate target of the stop and frisk as they accounted for over half the stops conducted by police. The funny part is, of the small percentage of the white community that were stopped, they were statistically more likely to have weapons on them.

Well, it all came to a head in 2013 after a federal judge ruled the NYPD's stop and frisk policy unconstitutional as it violated the fourth amendment. The NYPD was forced to make remedies to their policy. Of course the police unions pushed back and filed an appeal, but the decision stood, in theory at least. The NYPD is currently still accused of racial police tactics from the remnants of stop and frisk. They still have a ways to go to improve community relations.

CHAPTER EIGHT

DEFUND, REFORM, OR ABOLISH

There has been a movement lately to defund the police in many cities. Some even want them abolished altogether. I admit that due to recent events, it is extremely difficult to defend the actions of police right now. I can only offer a perspective that people will hopefully take into account before forming a hard opinion on the subject.

First, I will begin by saying I am against abolishing police. As bad as police look overall nowadays, abolishing police will not work. It is a dangerous concept. While most people would probably keep to themselves, there will be a segment of the population that would run buck wild. Without anyone to stop them or hold them accountable for their crimes, then innocent and defenseless people will be victimized. This reminds me of "*The Purge*" movie series. In each of those films, a day was set aside each year for the public to purge, or get out of their system any crime they wanted to commit. For that one day any crime was legal. The police and other first responders did not respond to any calls, and for that one night it was complete mayhem. People were forced to shelter-in-place until the time expired. If you lived to tell about it great; if not, there were no consequences and your family had to move on. It was just a movie and it was indeed exaggerated. If it were to occur in reality, the movie would not be far off base. I mean art reflects reality, right?

Without a police department, where do people turn to for immediate help? If a woman is getting abused by her spouse, who should she call? If a child goes missing, who looks for them? If there is a bad car wreck, who responds to investigate? There will be burglaries, robberies, and rapes that no one will look into. If you own a business and people disrupt your operation because they loiter, trespass, or harass your customers, what would you do? It's easy to say you will fight people off yourself. How can you run an effective business if your energy is focused elsewhere? Perhaps you will hire private security. That can easily lead to violence and lawsuits if your security team does not conduct itself appropriately. Not to mention you are taking away from your profits by hiring security. Then we will be in a situation where only the wealthy can afford to hire competent security, which is basically how the history of police started anyway. Wealthy plantation owners hired citizens to protect and collect their assets. If that happens, society would have come full circle putting us back at square one. Residents with resources will organize and create their "protection forces." Residents without resources will be at the mercy of those who do. It will essentially be police under a new name.

During the summer of 2020, there were protests around the country in many cities in response to the deaths of George Floyd and Breonna Taylor. Citizens in some cities established police-free autonomous zones. Seattle, in particular, established what was called "CHAZ" or Capital Hill Autonomous Zone. The people in that area set up barriers and restricted police from responding to the area. The police precinct in that area was abandoned and boarded up. That precinct was effectively "cancelled."

The CHAZ initially began pretty well. There were public events, festive music, and just an overall happy environment. Even the mayor of Seattle seemed to give her approval of it. Things took a turn as violence struck from within the CHAZ. A few shootings occurred in the area and two people were killed in less than two weeks. That should give many people a glimpse into what can happen if police are completely abolished.

The family of one of the people killed in the CHAZ has filed a lawsuit against the city citing negligence against first responders who failed to respond. Furthermore, a class action lawsuit from business owners in the CHAZ (which was later renamed CHOP or "Capital Hill Occupied Protest") also sued the city for lack of essential services as many owners had their places of business vandalized or their business disrupted since the CHOP was established. Although CHOP started off good in theory, it eventually devolved into an area of chaos and lawlessness. I recognize that many people have a negative sentiment towards police right now. I doubt anyone wants to be subjected to this type of atmosphere where there is no protection at all.

If the police department gets abolished, the law enforcement burden will fall on the sheriff's department. Unless they are abolished as well. Most people group the sheriff's department and police departments together anyway as they have similar functions. I assume when people say abolish police, they really mean law enforcement altogether. Some counties do not have a police department; they solely rely on their sheriff's department. In those such areas, sheriff's departments respond to calls, enforce traffic laws, and also manage the jail.

If the police were abolished, then technically the sheriff's department has to be abolished. If the sheriff's department weren't abolished, they would be too stressed out from picking up the slack of not having police and serving whole cities instead of only serving counties. If you do abolish the sheriff's department along with the police, then there is no one to manage the jails. You may as well release all prisoners at that point. Then you will have no one to serve restraining orders, child support summons, or any type of court subpoenas. There will definitely be no one to serve and carry out arrest warrants.

If you are a landlord and have tenants that need evicted, there will be no one to do that for you. At least no government entity will. At this point, all courts may as well shut their doors for good. What good is a court order if there is no one to enforce it? Any type of laws, rules, or regulations are only as good as the system in place to enforce it.

As I mentioned before, a person could privatize enforcement. Assuming you can afford it, you can hire a team of people, to perform certain functions for you, such as evictions. There will be nothing in place to keep the person evicted from retaliating against you. Society will turn into the survival of the financially fittest, even more so than it is now. Those who can afford to protect themselves, will. Everyone else will have to improvise. Even the mundane and minute tasks, such as filing a police report for stolen or lost property, will become a thing of the past. When it comes to replacing certain documents, like a missing driver's license or social security card, police reports are required.

My point is this, if police departments are totally abolished, holes will be left in our society. The real criminals will never be caught or punished. Yes, there is "street justice," but you won't find many people who want to put their lives at risk for free. Police officers get paid to be in harm's way; yet, we still get apprehensive. In addition to this issue, there will be a whole sector of jobs lost. There are currently anywhere between 700,000 - 800,000 police officers in the country. If that many people lost their jobs, some would likely become the very criminals they are used to putting in jail.

I am not claiming to have all the answers, but abolishing police probably won't work due to the reasons I just stated. For those advocating for abolishment I would like to hear resolutions to everything I just mentioned, and not just emotional testimony, because it will take much more than emotion to get the black community justice.

DEFUNDING

Defunding the police is the next level before complete abolishment. I am definitely open to this concept as long as it can be done responsibly. By that I mean if there is room in the budget to cut funds without police officers taking a pay cut, sacrificing training, or hurting manpower, then it should be done.

No cop wants to take a pay cut or have their days furloughed. The job is already hard and stressful enough, and many of us feel we are generally underpaid. We have a right to earn a living and support our families just like any other profession. If the police were defunded to the point where we either had to take a pay decrease or never get a raise, many would quit and communities everywhere would suffer. Response times will increase and the job would become ever more dangerous. This would lead even more cops quitting leaving an untenable cycle.

As far as training is concerned, both advocates and critics to law enforcement agree more training is needed. Training is needed on de-escalation tactics, it is needed on crisis intervention to help deal with the mentally ill, as well as for defensive tactics. Perhaps more training with self-defense maneuvers will lead to fewer officer involved shootings. Training is essential and essential means it is also not free. Training involves time and resources provided by experienced instructors, held at quality facilities, and with updated equipment and technology, none of which is free. If the police department were to be defunded, then training cannot be cut. The budget cuts have to come from a different area.

I can also argue that more time is needed in the police academy before graduating. In Finland and Norway, prospecting police officers have to attend what is tantamount to a university. The officers in those countries learn and study policing for three years before they graduate. Here in America, a recruit can become a sworn police officer in a fraction of the time. The police academy I went through was just over five months. Most major police departments have their academy run about six months. Here in Georgia, however, basic law enforcement mandate school is only twelve weeks! A person in that academy can become a police officer over the summer. This pales in comparison to Finland's academy. In case you are wondering, Finland only had seven people killed by police between the years 2000-2018. Seems to me like Finland's training works. If we can defund police, then training has to not only stay, it has to increase.

I personally want to see police defunded which would allow us not to respond to certain calls. Small fender-bender accidents should not require police. A non-violent, mentally ill person suffering a behavior health crisis who asks for an ambulance should not require a police response. Any type of low priority call, typically any call where no violence or quality of life issue is alleged, should be outsourced. This way the police stay available to handle higher priority calls, and the public will not have to worry about response time. More importantly, encounters with the police would decrease, so would the chances of a deadly encounter. Both the citizens and the police are safer that way.

REFORM

Police reform has been a major topic for decades, especially now given recent events. What exactly is reform? What does it look like? How will reform come about? Which police departments need reformed? These are all questions that need answering if reform is going to happen. Many people say reform is needed, but no one has a concrete solution of how to do it. I hear politicians use the phrase police reform when they are campaigning for election. Police reform seems to only be lip service from politicians or a buzz word to stir momentum among their voting base. I don't think most politicians have any idea how to go about police reform. If they did, reform would have already happened.

Webster's definition of reform is "to improve; abandon evil practices, reconstruct." I find the 'abandon evil practices' part amusing since many people currently see police as the bad guys anyway; sometimes for good reason. Law enforcement everywhere needs to consistently improve. Almost every other aspect of society improves over time. Technology, medicine, and communications are a few things that improve over time, policing should be one of them. It just needs to improve with the safety of the public and police officer in mind.

Exactly how do we reform policing? That is the

million-dollar question. As I mentioned before, it needs to start with more training from the onset. America should mimic what Finland and Norway do in regards to extensive training. Let's think about it, a doctor requires years of studying and training before they become a licensed physician. An attorney must complete years of study before passing the bar exam. Certified electricians can spend a year in training, and the list goes on. Ten thousand hours is the proverbial benchmark for mastering a subject or discipline. If a person commits ten thousand hours towards a specific task, then it is safe to say that person is at least adequate in that field. For example, if a police academy is 40 hours per week, then it will take 62 weeks, or just over a year, to get a handle on policing. Most police academies last far less than a year.

It is time to stop treating law enforcement like any other run-of-the-mill career, and actually dedicate the training it needs and deserves. This is not the 1970s or 80s anymore where three or four months of training will suffice. Laws have evolved, people have evolved, technology has evolved, and society overall is different.

Law enforcement needs to adapt to the times. I can't name many professions besides law enforcement where a life-or-death decision is made in a matter of seconds, sometimes split seconds. The only profession that comes to mind is the military, and the military trains constantly.

Sworn law enforcement officers are required to complete annual training, but it pales in comparison to active military. De-escalation has been a big emphasis of late, but de-escalation may not always work. Responding to a school shooting in progress, a chance to de-escalate may not present itself if there are suspects with automatic weapons involved. There are dozens of situations where de-escalation tactics won't be an option, the point is to use them whenever possible.

Along with de-escalation training, more training in defensive tactics will help. Training in some form of martial arts will also be beneficial. Imagine if all police officers graduated from the police academy with a black belt in karate, jujitsu, or some other form of martial arts. The use of deadly force would decrease as cops gain more preparation and confidence to apprehend criminals that resisted arrest. I have a co-worker who is a martial arts expert. He suggested to our command staff that at the very least to help with defensive tactics, that the gym be converted into a room where officers can practice grappling techniques and take down maneuvers. My co-worker's emails were ignored and his idea never came to fruition.

Ultimately, for true reform to occur, other entities outside of the police will need to participate. Those other entities include the police unions and the government. For true reform to occur, police unions need to get involved.

POLICE UNIONS

Police unions have a history of opposing citizen review boards, restrictive department policies, and legislation that promotes police accountability. Unions insist the general public is not knowledgeable enough to weigh in on policy. Unions also give undeserving bad cops a form of due process when an incident occurs. Too many times a cop has engaged in egregious behavior, but their department is slow or hesitant to terminate them. Police unions are the reason. Until the process plays out, the chief or other top personnel has no power to do anything other than wait. That is because these unions have power and their pockets are deep. Many police unions make financial contributions to political campaigns. Even after someone is elected to office, the political contributions continue to roll in which influence reform against police or the lack thereof. A smart politician will not bite the hand that feeds them, so they essentially go along with the status quo. Until politicians refuse contributions from police unions, then do not expect any real reform to happen.

Most police officers are part some type of union, myself included. As with any other profession, police unions advocate on the behalf of cops across the country. They push for pay raises, better working conditions, and legislation that favors the police. They also provide legal representation. I won't vilify a cop simply because they choose to be in a union since they are only looking out for their personal best interest. I just do not believe all police unions advocate with the best interest of the community at heart. I chose not to become a member of the Fraternal Order of Police, one the most popular unions, because of their public stance on some of the police killings that have occurred in recent past. Unions are slow to criticize or excoriate cops who break the law or those who don't uphold the professional standard of policing.

A few years ago, a football player named Colin Kaepernick decided to kneel for the national anthem. The reason he took a knee was in protest against police brutality and racial injustice. I, for one, was not offended. I was in support of Kaepernick's stance because police brutality is an issue that affects the black community more than others. It also affects the safety of good police officers. However, many police officers and departments across the country took issue with Kaepernick's stance.

The Santa Clara Police Officer's Association, the union representing Santa Clara Police that patrols during San Francisco 49er home games, sent a letter to the 49ers expressing their disdain for Kaepernick's protest and even threatened to boycott working 49er games unless

Kaepernick was disciplined. That union was willing to risk the safety and protection of taxpayers based on a stance without logic, reason, or understanding. That union wasn't alone either. Police unions in Florida also made it known they were willing to boycott working games when players on the Miami Dolphins began taking a knee.

Every police officer and police department should be against police brutality. If Kaepernick's stance doesn't apply to you, then it shouldn't bother you. Kaepernick's opinion is just that, an opinion, and he is entitled to have one. You don't have to agree or like it, but to try and change the narrative as if Kaepernick attacked or insulted all police is actually irresponsible. Also, let's not forget that while Kaerpernick was protesting during the season, a presidential campaign was in full swing. While on the campaign trail, Donald Trump spewed rhetoric that implied police officers should be physically rougher with criminals. I didn't hear any police unions push back on his comments. This double standard is exactly why police can't shake the racist stigma.

I chose to join a union simply to have legal protection while performing my duties. The job is extremely high risk. Too many incidents can happen while performing in the line of duty to go without counsel. I personally find it in my best interest to have representation in the event I have to use deadly force, because it is a real possibility in this line of work. Even in a justified shooting, there will be a media storm and critics from the community. I really can't blame the public at this point because law enforcement has lost all benefit of the doubt.

CHAPTER NINE

DEVIL'S ADVOCATE

Being that I am a black cop, many times I see incidents from two perspectives. Sometimes those perspectives are in agreement, other times they are not. Some of these high-profile events where black men are killed make me look from two perspectives. First, I ask myself if race played a factor. Sometimes, I believe it does.

When Michael Slager shot and killed Walter Scott in South Carolina in 2015, I definitely believe race was a factor. I seriously doubt Slager would shoot a white man who was running away in the back, then plant his taser as evidence and lie about what happened. If not for a cell phone video taken by a bystander, Slager may have gotten away with it. Let's not forget the first trial ended in a mistrial, so Slager still almost got away with it. Luckily justice prevailed and Slager was convicted.

The second question I ask myself is more from a cop-like perspective. I ask myself would I have done the same thing in a similar situation. That question is a bit more complicated to answer because I am dealing with 20/20 hindsight vision. You really have to put yourself in that officer's shoes and imagine you only knew what he or she knew at that moment. Remember, I told you earlier that when a cop unjustly shoots someone, it is because they are being racist, scared, or stupid. And by scared, I mean unnecessarily scared. You're not human if you don't get scared or anxious in some situations. If I respond to bank robbery in progress with three suspects all armed with assault rifles, then you can trust and believe I'd be scared. I'll still respond to the call, but you get the picture. Being unnecessarily scared is being afraid of a suspect simply because of his or her race. If the cop was not being racist, scared, or stupid, then that likely means they acted within the scope of the law and actually reacted to a credible threat.

I think back to the Rayshard Brooks incident that happened in Atlanta in June of 2020. This incident occurred on the heels of the deaths of George Floyd and Breonna Taylor, so the country was already at its wits end. Mr. Brooks was killed by Atlanta Police officers after an attempted arrest quickly went bad. It started with a simple call to police about a man asleep at the wheel at a Wendy's drive-thru which turned into an investigation for driving under the influence. From that was born a deadly use of force after the police tried to place Mr. Brooks in handcuffs.

The mood of the general public is that Mr. Brooks should not have gotten killed. I hate what happened to Mr. Brooks, but I understand why deadly force was used in that situation. I asked myself did race play a role in his death. I know there were two white cops trying to arrest Mr. Brooks, who is black, but I did not get the sense that race was a factor. I then asked myself if I would have done the same thing in the same situation, and I probably would have.

If Mr. Brooks would have run away without taking the taser, I would have tried to chase him down and put him in handcuffs. But, if he would have taken my taser and actually pointed it at me the way he did those officers, then yes, I would have to use deadly force. At that point it comes down to self-preservation. If I get shot in the face or neck with a taser, then I could very well die. Police are trained not to shoot tasers at certain areas of the body. Since Mr. Brooks is not a trained police officer, I doubt he knew any better. Therefore, I can't be mad at those cops for doing something I would have done if I were in their position.

The cops involved in that incident, Devin Brosnan and Garrett Rolfe, were fired from their department and also charged with murder within days of the incident. Public sentiment would say those cops would not have been charged if they did nothing wrong, however, I disagree. I believe there were political motives behind those charges. The district attorney at the time, Paul Howard, was running for re-election. What better way to cater to your constituents than to charge police officers at a critical time in our country where policing is under a microscope? I don't believe Mr. Howard was sure he could actually win this case. He just wanted the votes. The election occurred later that fall, months before a trial actually took place. If Mr. Howard would have won the upcoming election, then he would have achieved his objective and figured out the rest later.

This is the same district attorney who charged six Atlanta cops with aggravated assault in connection with two young college kids being stopped and tasered a few weeks prior to the Rayshard Brooks incident. Many in the law enforcement community feel the six cops should not have been charged. I do believe the cops in that situation overreacted and allowed their egos to dictate what happened instead of rationale and safe practices; however, the charges seemed a bit excessive. The new district attorney will have a tough time trying that case in court.

I wanted to touch on those above situations because justice has to be consistent. When white, racist police officers kill black people without justifiable means, then they should be held accountable. Conversely, overcharging cops in criminal cases, whether black or white, will not make up for the dozens, if not hundreds of times the cops were either undercharged or not charged altogether when innocent black lives were killed.

SOLUTIONS

How exactly do we make sure this country has

effective policing while not subjugating the black community? Honestly, I don't have any concrete answers, only opinions and suggestions. I can tell you that true reform is nearly impossible. Fair and equitable policing are not guaranteed in this current system. The black community will not experience the privileges bestowed upon the elite of our society; therefore, reform as the rest of the general public wants it is off the table.

If the powers that be actually had an interest in making noticeable and sustainable changes, they need to start with who becomes a cop. As mentioned before, law enforcement needs to recruit and retain quality, competent people who are generally unbiased and definitely not racist or bigoted. That is easier said than done, especially when police departments either miss or ignore red flags during the hiring process. There needs to be a deeper dive into the ideology and upbringing of some of these cops. Potential black police officers have a higher threshold to cross during the hiring process compared to white cops. This is especially true when the police department they are looking to get hired with is majority white. For white cops, they look for a reason to hire them; for black cops, they look for reasons *not* to hire them. Still, I strongly encourage our black men and women to join police departments because representation does matter.

I would like to see police recruits interviewed by a citizen review board before they are hired. Citizen review boards typically operate in a reactive context. They review and investigate complaints or allegations on cops after the fact. All potential candidates should go before the review board twice: once before the academy begins and once again after it is over before they are assigned to patrol. This way, citizens have a say in who gets to work in their communities. The review board should be allowed to see a candidate's social media to look for anything detrimental to him or her working in any law enforcement capacity. Anything on social media that suggests biasness towards a group of people or ties to any hate group should deem that candidate not hirable.

Potential candidates should also be exposed to the communities they will serve prior to being hired.

Candidates should be required to perform some type of community service in the areas they will eventually work. The first day wearing a badge and gun should not be the first time an officer sets foot in that community. Whether it is volunteering at an elementary school, feeding the homeless, or participating in a community event, that candidate should have to indoctrinate themselves into that community. That candidate should be required to spend a pre-determined number of hours serving that community before he or she actually "serves" the community.

The black community also needs a private union, or advocacy group, to combat the police unions. This black advocacy group needs a financial base to compete against the police unions, especially when it comes to donating to politicians and their campaigns. That is when we will begin to see real results, real reform. Politicians currently have no incentive to heed the demands for police reform from the black community. With an advocacy group, we can financially entice politicians to pass legislation on our behalf. We can also punish the bad cops without all the red tape. Justice will come down swift and harsh.

In conclusion, whatever changes that occur within law enforcement will happen over time. Too many bad seeds and corrupt ideology still exist. When the Department of Justice has investigated dozens of major police agencies and found similar cases of injustice and unconstitutional policing, America definitely has a problem. And it's clear that the problem is not isolated to a particular agency or area. This problem has taken root and permeated itself throughout law enforcement. I hope this book has awakened the conscious of police agencies so change can occur swiftly and permanently.

I understand if you disagree with the concepts I have presented. Just understand that most of this book is based on documented facts, not conjecture. At the end of the day, I am not an esteemed scholar, but I do have eyes, ears, and a perspective from my own experiences. This is what makes me qualified to speak on this issue. Some of my law enforcement colleagues will openly agree with me and what I have presented; others will agree only in secret. There are others who will vehemently disagree.

Some will have a logical basis for their varying opinion, but others will disagree just because they want to be contrary. Some will disagree because they want to protect the racist status quo of law enforcement. Just know that I'm okay with every scenario. I will sleep easy at night knowing I have done my part to improve not only my community, but how this country polices going forward.

ACKNOWLEDGEMENTS

First, I must acknowledge and thank The Most High God for allowing me to complete this project. I had doubts about doing this, and for some time I put it off. After a while, I was just overwhelmed to see it through, and I have Him to thank for that. We all have purpose in this life. I hope and pray this book was part of my purpose for being here.

Next, I would like to thank my family. I want to thank the incredible woman in my life, Koji. She is the definition of loyal and is what a true support system looks like. Even when she's mad at me, she still carries on and makes sure I'm good. What's funny is that if I had not become a cop, I may not have met her. So, for that reason alone, I don't regret becoming a police officer.

I also would like to thank my children, Khalil and Kylie, who are the motivation behind everything. Both my son, who is the oldest, and my baby girl knew I was writing this book, but they probably did not understand the weight of it. They both are aware of police killings in the news that happened over the recent years. They definitely know about the killing of George Floyd that sent shock waves around the world.

With childlike innocence and curiosity, they ask questions about what they saw and heard. As a parent, I provided the best answers I could, hoping they understood. I try not to sugarcoat anything because the harsh reality is that either one of them can end up in an encounter with the police. Even if they have not done anything wrong, a chance encounter with police can go sideways. Even the parents who shelter their children from certain events were forced to address the George Floyd event with their kids.

Call it PTSD, or a "hope for the best but prepare for the worst" mentality, but every black parent in America needs to have their children prepared with knowledge, information, and most important of all, a plan, for if they are stopped by the police.

I want to thank my dad, Kelvin Collins, who sparked my interest in reading and books. As a kid, I sat on his lap as he read to me, then eventually I began reading to him when I learned enough. I thank my brothers, KJ and Ron, and my sister, Khelsea. We've cracked enough jokes on each other to probably fill a book. That sense of humor is what kept my mind loose enough to finish this book and not take myself too seriously. I also want to thank my cousins and close friends who supported me and gave me inspiration to write this book as well.

Along with my family, I want to thank some of the really good cops I know who will never turn their back on their community. My man, Jeff Churchill, who works in Atlanta is one of the cops who inspired me to become one. I want to thank officers David Jackson, Kevin Williams, Devon Perry, and other cops who know how to police and also have an understanding of people. Of course, there are others, but it's too many to name. I appreciate all the good cops who have served with integrity.

To all the bad cops out there.... your day is coming.

EPILOGUE

There's something inherently brave about being black in America

Imagine living in that truth, then taking an oath to protect and serve in that same country, Hero

To stand in the middle of the storm and try to calm the winds

These pages were written without fear even when surrounded by it

The fear of condemnation

The fear of failure

The fear of death

True freedom comes with absolute honesty

Honesty about the fears that motivate us all

This is a journey of enlightenment

Illuminating the blackness in a blue wall of silence

-By Mario J Menina

REFERENCES

- *The Black and The Blue: A Cop Reveals the Crimes, Racism, and Injustice in America's Law Enforcement*; by Matthew Horace Black
- *Black and Blue*: *Inside the Divide Between The Police and Black America*; by Jeff Pegues
- *Breaking Rank: A Top Cop's Expose of the Dark Side of American Policing*; by Norm Stamper
- *I Know My Rights*; by David W. Jackson
- *Georgia Law Enforcement Handbook Criminal Law & Procedure*
- https://documents.latimes.com/tamir-rice-investigation-part-1/
- https://www.washingtonpost.com/news/post-nation/wp/2017/06/21/what-the-police-officer-who-shot-philando-castile-said-about-the-shooting/
- https://www.startribune.com/read-the-transcript-of-officer-jeronimo-yanez-s-bca-interview/429665063/?TB_iframe=true&height=658.8&width=370.8
- https://tulsaworld.com/news/shooting-of-

terence-crutcher-in-tulsa-the-tulsa-world-archive/collection_be8a61d0-77ff-58f4-8c65-7292672bac5a.html#16

- https://www.cnn.com/2019/06/07/us/minneapolis-mohamed-noor-sentenced
- https://time.com/5628206/police-shooting-trial-knowlton-garner/
- https://www.msn.com/en-us/news/us/identity-crisis-white-supremacist-racist-american-cops-must-be-removed-experts-say-it-will-take-resolve/ar-BB1eT90J?ocid=uxbndlbing
- https://www.washingtonpost.com/news/opinions/wp/2018/11/02/feature/if-you-dont-get-at-that-rot-you-just-get-more-officers-like-josh-hastings/
- https://www.nbcnews.com/news/us-news/two-louisiana-cops-arrested-fatal-shooting-boy-6-n459136
- https://www.chicagoreporter.com/ex-officer-shot-28-times-deserves-justice/

Keep in touch!

@theconsciouscop

@theconsciouscop